Reconstructing Reality

Amy L. Rosner

Outsmarting the Brain to Rewrite Our Life Stories

Amy L. Rosner

Reconstructing Reality: Outsmarting the Brain to Rewrite Our Life Stories

copyright © 2024 Amy L. Rosner

All rights reserved.

No part of this publication may be reproduced, distributed, or transmitted in any form or by any means, including photocopying, recording, or other electronic or mechanical methods, without the prior written permission of the publisher, except in the case of brief quotations embodied in critical reviews and certain other noncommercial uses permitted by copyright law.

The resources in this book are provided for informational purposes only and should not be used to replace the specialized training and professional judgment of a health care or mental-health care professional.

Neither the author nor the publisher can be held responsible for the use of the information provided within this book. Please always consult a trained professional before making any decision regarding treatment of yourself or others.

ISBN: 979-8-89109-777-3 - hardcover

ISBN: 979-8-89109-778-0 - paperback

ISBN: 979-8-89109-779-7 - ebook

Published by Amy Rosner, LLC

For more information, bulk orders, signed copies, and speaking engagements, email info@amyrosner.com.

Cover design by Joice Panilagao

Edited by Margaret A. Harrell

Get relaxation in your inbox

by joining our free private online community, the Stretch & Smile Club, for support, Q&A, group challenges, meetups, . . . and tips, tricks, and ninja sneak attacks on the brain to help you reduce stress, stay positive, and live your best life

<https://www.amyrosner.com/signup>

. . . also, enjoy a free hypnosis recording for a relaxing emotional reboot anytime during your day to keep you clear-headed, creative, and productive

For all researchers and practitioners from all backgrounds and orientations—past, present, and yet to be—who are driven by the desire to help others live their best lives.

Contents

Introduction	IX
1. You Versus Your Brain	1
2. Birth of a Block	15
3. How the Brain Works	25
4. Hemispheric Asymmetries and Consciousness	43
5. Outsmarting the Brain	59
6. Hypnotherapy	73
7. Benefits of Hypnotherapy and Related Protocols	89
8. Outcomes of an Unconscious-Oriented Approach	101
Acknowledgements	115
What people are saying...	117
Also By Amy L. Rosner	121
Thank You!	123
Endnotes	124

Introduction

As I write this book, I am in my bed with my laptop on my lap and my pit bull, Duke, plastered to my right hip (the "pit" stands for "pitiful"—he has epic snuggling needs), and I am full of feelings that I can barely control about my vacation to France, coming up in a few days. For forty years, I've waited for this trip. I went there as an exchange student in high school and loved everyone I met and everything I saw. It was almost inconceivably magical. On that trip I flew into Paris Orly Airport but left almost immediately for the Gare de Lyon train station—only able to glance at the Eiffel Tower briefly out of the bus window. Then on to Grenoble, my ultimate destination, where my amazing French family awaited. What I did not see in Paris: any of the museums or monuments the artist in me longed to; did not eat in any restaurants or even have a café au lait in a charming bistro, and did not drink any of their famous Burgundy or Bordeaux wines. But I was experiencing real French life, which most Americans are not lucky enough to see, and I knew that one day I would make it back to do the touristy stuff. That is just a few days off.

I can barely stand the anticipation. When I made a cup of tea this morning, it came with delicious flashbacks of the tea I had every morning for breakfast with my French family and my life-changing introduction to Nutella on my toast. I can taste it now.

I have limited success telling myself to not be distracted by those images and feelings so I can concentrate on what I want to get done now, before leaving. It seems most of my mind and body are halfway to France already. Technically speaking, I can tell you that unconscious processes in my brain drive those feelings by communicating with me, using images, emotions, and body sensations. I like to think I can rationally control what I'm thinking about and paying attention to, but those excited feelings are always there, right under the surface, and pop up gloriously into my awareness whenever my hubby and I talk about packing our suitcases or what snacks we're going to take on the plane. And those feelings include not just excitement about this journey, but warm memories of discovery and affection from my first visit there as well as cruises we've taken with the good friends we'll be traveling with. Remarkably clear images and feelings of those past trips—playing cards, laughing until our sides hurt, admiring chateaux and the beautiful French countryside with awe—are bombarding me throughout the day today.

At times like this, I understand just how powerful our unconscious brain processes are and how many memories, with their images, emotions, and physical feelings, associate with one another in my brain. These memories and feelings are not just fleeting mental events; they have changed the structure of my brain and will change it even more as my brain uses that information to predict how my highly anticipated experiences will go and then later incorporates information from the new experiences into that neural network concerned with France and cruises and vacations and friends and other concepts and memories more distantly and weakly linked, like the ripples of a drop of water into a still pool.

I have always viewed thoughts and emotions as physical brain events and wanted to know more about how changing them could impact me, you—all of us—psychologically and physically. *I believed that mind over matter was a real thing.* So when, early on in my career, I had the opportunity to test that belief with an objective measure of physical responses, I jumped at the chance.

Having applied for a job as a police officer, I was required to take a lie detector test. *I'm usually such a rule follower. But some little devil on my shoulder made me want to see if I could use a single change of thought to beat the polygraph machine.* During the baseline test, I had to pick a number between one and ten, write it on a piece of paper, and sit on it. I repeated, "Five, five, five, five, . . ." over and over silently but wrote the number "two"—as quickly and with as little attention as possible—on the piece of paper; then I sat on it, continuing to repeat "five" to myself. Asking me if my number was one, then two, etc.—through ten—the interviewer observed my physiological responses. With each answer, he looked at the machine, then at me, then back at the machine, then at me again, and finally said, "What did you do?"

"What do you mean?" I asked, straight-faced.

"The machine says your number is five."

It worked! I was elated. I had fooled the machine. The interviewer, however, was not so easily outsmarted. "But I think it's two," he said astutely.

I was deeply intrigued that I beat the machine *but not the interviewer*. I told him what I did, and he had never heard of such a trick. He was impressed. "You should work here with me, and we should go to conferences together," he immediately suggested. I may be the only person ever to have had an awesome time taking a lie detector test.

I was only a police officer for, like, five minutes. By training, I'm a brain scientist with a PhD in Experimental Psychology with a major in Biopsychology and a minor in Experimental Neuropsychology. Many years back, I spent my days doing laboratory research focused on inferring brain function from partial brain damage: what is known as "experimental neuropsychology." My research focused on *localization of function*; in other words, I investigated which brain functions were affected by damage to different parts of the brain. In particular, visual attention and memory.

But back to the lie detector test. *For some time I'd toyed with the idea that I could change my physiology mentally—just by thinking about it.* That is, suppose I wanted to lower my blood pressure. *Could I do that just by thinking it was lower?* My little polygraph machine experiment provided some evidence that it was possible and worth looking into further.

I could change the lie detector result only so much, though, because I beat the machine but not the man interpreting what the machine was telling him. When we engage in deceit, our respiratory and heart rates increase, we start to sweat, our mouth goes dry, and our voice can shake, some or all of which the interviewer picked up on. From his years of giving polygraph tests, he could identify my lie, whereas the machine could not. His radar was more sensitive than the machine.

Still, it was fascinating to me that with only a simple thought I could make that much of a change in my body's physiology—whether in heart rate, skin conductance, or any or all of the measures the polygraph records—in such a short time. So first of all, the audience I was playing to was my body. It had to believe the lie.

If I could do that much, what other physical and mental changes were possible? I had no idea then just how life changing that question would be years later, after I discovered my calling and began helping people *rewrite* their stories. Yes, by applying this same technique, you can rewire your brain and rewrite what the future holds.

As you can guess, I did not make policework my career. I first entered the academic world, heavily involving myself in research. However, I soon grew disillusioned. The research world, which brought with it the prospect of teaching the same classes every semester for the next thirty years, made me feel like I was dying a slow death. My brain was too packed with ideas to continue in that direction, so I left academia and tried different professions, including the aforementioned brief stint at policework. Ultimately, though, psychology was where my heart was, and I still had much to learn from it. I knew it. How could I get back into it in a way that really interested me? excited me?

After a marvelous, rewarding experience with a life coach, I determined to be one myself. This was counterintuitive to my past assumptions. I had never resonated with the psychotherapy premise that I could help "fix" broken or mentally ill people. I thought "symptoms" of such disorders might just be evidence of the brain doing its protective healing work. I wondered: *could changing those protection (or survival) programs lead to changes in thoughts, feelings, and behaviors? And could these shifts be physiological?* Couldn't individuals, with the intent of making improvements, remake aspects of themselves with some easy brain hacks—using clever techniques to tap into how the brain worked—like I did with the polygraph test? Yes. Why not?

But I hadn't been a coach for long before I realized that rational ways of hacking the brain could take people only so far. Even if they could deal better with a particular difficulty, the issue was still there. I wanted to *pull the weed out by the root* so my clients would never be impacted by that issue again and could move forward with whatever they wanted to do in life faster and more easily. So I started using *brain hacks directed at unconscious processes*. My clients' successes skyrocketed.

Imagine my surprise when a client who had come to me to stop smoking just a week before told me she had *forgotten to smoke that week*. From my work in an addiction lab in graduate school, I always had the impression that such brains were essentially hijacked by a chemical, so I was astounded to hear her statement. When I reflected, however, it made sense. Thoughts, feelings, and behaviors are ultimately chemical events in the brain, and these internal chemical events impact us as much as external chemicals, such as nicotine.

In fact, the reason we are affected by the chemicals in cigarette smoke or drugs of abuse or medications is because we have receptors for those chemicals in our brains. We have receptors for them because we *make* a version of those chemicals ourselves. Then we release them when we think, feel, and do things. *Outside influences would not affect us if our brains were not already physically structured to do the same things for us*. We have more control over our brains than we tend to think; we just have to outsmart our brain sometimes—get sneaky with it—using unconsciously oriented brain hacks to make changes that our rational, conscious minds think we can't.

Why did that client forget to smoke, even with an addiction to dosing herself with nicotine on a frequent basis? Because during the previous session we discovered—and eliminated—a need she had *that was not about smoking* but about belonging. She was using the perceived comfort of smoking to feel better about being away from her friends after moving to a new place. When she missed that sense of belonging in the moment, she grabbed a cigarette. For a few moments it worked—she felt better—but it did not change the underlying need for belonging, itself. Once we addressed the need, she didn't need to be comforted anymore; the smoking behavior stopped. It may sound miraculous and unbelievable, but I assure you, that is the powerful hold an unconscious feeling can have.

How many products on the market are advertised to help people stop smoking? How much money do people pay to try to facilitate that change, and how often does it not happen or not stick? Now comes the best part of the story: one session was enough. Believable or not on the surface, it's an absolute fact. She didn't need more than that to curtail that behavior.

Changes at the unconscious level, bypassing the rational mind, are not only biochemical, they are also structural. Unlike taking a medication, such as applying a nicotine patch (which only impacts the person as long as she continues to use the drug), to have a one-and-done solution, you must change something physically. Medication, by contrast, creates a temporary chemical availability. More medication has to be used to continue feeling its effects.

Techniques that bypass the rational mind can provide enormous benefits. These techniques *tap directly into unconscious processes by which our brain constantly reconstructs our memories and concepts.*

That's a major focus of this book, something I became aware of in working with *thousands* of clients. Simple changes occur quickly, and more complex modifications come over time. With regular sessions utilizing these techniques in a coaching setting, clients are able to *get on their A-game and stay on it as they intentionally reconstruct their memories and psychological concepts to improve their interactions with the world*. That's the brain's job—predicting what experiences we will have and then, if and when those predictions are not quite accurate, modifying our neural connections. The techniques I use are not like waving a magic wand; rather, they are hacks that tap into that reconstruction process.

One of my first clients—let's call her Maria—came to me, distressed over issues at work. "I cannot focus on anything or remember what anyone tells me," she admitted, embarrassed and deflated. Her coworkers, she knew, were not able to appreciate all she had to offer, and a superior even told her that she would never make manager. As it turned out, Maria grew up with an abusive father, and her relationships were all with similarly dangerous men. She lived in fear daily, both from her controlling boyfriend and from her traumatic memories. With shattered self-esteem, she felt completely unworthy of getting anything in life she wanted. She had failed at everything, which, according to her boyfriend and boss both, was because she wasn't smart enough.

Eight years of monthly sessions later, Maria is not only a manager but also a program developer, interacting with her local community on behalf of her company, and sits on local government committees to help improve her city. Previously unable to pass a math class to get her college degree, she has aced several math courses and is about to start working toward a graduate degree. Finally beginning to fulfill her lifelong passion of being an entrepreneur, Maria is developing her own nonprofit to help victims of domestic violence. With her entire self-concept revitalized, she is also healthier physically, and her gastric issues occur now only if she finds herself under a hefty load of stress.

One of the brain hacks that helped her was hypnotherapy. Many people are surprised that it and other brain hacks can let us reconstruct our memories and concepts, changing them the way we want to—rewriting our life stories. They allow us to rid ourselves of fear from traumatic memories and limiting beliefs like unworthiness. Often I am a last resort for desperate people. They have tried everything to no avail. When they leave my office feeling better, sometimes completely back to normal, they are astounded. Whether it's a smoking issue, loneliness, a sense of not belonging, past trauma—you name it—that secret underlying saboteur can be rooted out by this strategy. If I had a dime for every time I've heard a client say something along the lines of, "Why wasn't I told about this years ago?" I'd have an awful lot of dimes. Hypnotherapy in particular has had a bad rap as a pseudoscience, which is incorrect. There is a good, reputable body of research, especially in the medical literature, showing its benefits as a tool to help people feel and heal better and to change their behavior to better serve them. I also use other unconsciously oriented protocols, such as neurolinguistic programming (NLP), imagery, and mindfulness to hack the brain in dramatic ways and help a client restore balance to the entire organism, mind and body, that is them.

I feel that the ten years I've been doing hypnotherapy have expanded my understanding of brain function in ways that could not have happened had I stayed in research. I still look to science to keep me up to date, but I am now also informed by anecdotal data and trends I see repeatedly in my clients. I use these trends to help them get more control over their brains, which would not work if those trends were not real and meaningful.

The purpose of writing this book is to share those trends and to illustrate how well they complement the neuroscience literature. They fit nicely with the modern reconstructive view of brain function—that is, that the brain constructs and then constantly reconstructs our memories and concepts in light of our experiences—as well as with research on the differences between the right and left hemispheres of the brain; actually, the cerebrum. My hope is to give the techniques I learned a seat at the table as an attractive option to use either along with or as an alternative to more typical medical and psychotherapy options, as this unconsciously directed approach resonates, sometimes more than those other options, with many people. Though different, they can be an equally effective way to utilize the striking fact that *thoughts and feelings are transformative chemical and structural events*. Knowing this, we can provide real solutions for maladaptive interactions.

I want this book to start a dialog, pure and simple. I'm not asking anyone to agree with me that unconsciously based interventions are the best first choice for all people wanting to make changes in how they think, feel, or act. I just want everyone to understand that these interventions are an option—a powerful one, at that. This book will explore the brain changes made by these techniques and illustrate that misinformation bars many people from utilizing this remarkably helpful group of ninja sneak attacks on the unconscious mental machinery that runs our lives. *I want to take the discussion past the assumptions that hypnotherapy doesn't work or only works for "suggestible" or weak-minded people, or that it's brainwashing or quackery. The serious—even transformational—impacts of these brain hacks make sense in terms of neuroplasticity, or changing neural connections.*

Having success with hypnotherapy and other protocols I discuss does not require a leap of faith, but rather an openness to the idea that thoughts, feelings, and behaviors make changes in the brain. And that by tapping into how the brain works, we can apply strategies that result in desired changes. Not a synthetic or contrived substance or process, hypnotherapy *naturally* creates results. As I explain, it's really an educational process, in which we learn how to *listen* to our real selves and get real control over our minds rather than feeling like our minds are controlling us. Ironically, the side effects of these protocols are positive, such as increased self-confidence, better sleep, and decreased stress, as each healing change ripples through the associated memories and concepts in our heads. And these sessions can be a lot of fun.

Chapter One

You Versus Your Brain

As my plane taxis down the tarmac to take off for France, I can't help but think of one of my favorite clients of all time and how his unconscious brain programming turned what would be amazing, fun adventures into *flights of terror*. Seven-year-old Jake was afraid of flying and heights, and he was becoming just as afraid of crowds. Because he was so scared all the time, he carried a blanket with him everywhere, like Linus, the *Peanuts* cartoon character, with his security blanket that he could not live without. My young client had tried mightily to control his fear, but nothing worked. This incredible kid decided he was going to find a solution to the problem, so he got online and did some research. Deciding he needed hypnotherapy, Jake had his mother bring him into my office. He walked in, clutching his blanket with a very determined expression on his face—a look of courage and strength amid constant fear. I asked his mother how I could help.

"Don't ask me," she said. "I'm just the driver." Jake filled me in. With his family about to go on vacation, he didn't want to be left behind because of the flying; also, there was the walkway in the destination airport, which was really high off of the ground.

I explained to Jake about a superpower he possessed called his unconscious mind and walked him through using it to get rid of his fear. At the end of the first session, the discomfort he experienced in his body whenever he even *thought about* flying or heights had vanished. At the end of the second session he told me, "I just don't feel afraid anymore. I can go anywhere and be just fine."

Entering my office for just his third session, he said, "Look, no blanket!" As that session ended, his nervousness at bay, he felt excited to go on vacation. He felt in control of his feelings because he understood how to use his superpower by using the mental tools I gave him.

A year later his mom sent me a picture of him looking down from the top of the Empire State Building, smiling.

Another year or two passed and he informed his mother that his superpower was failing him. Could he come in for another session? Having to give a solo performance in a musical group at school, he just couldn't shake the stage fright. But after one session, gone was the apprehension. He was good to go. His mother sent me a video of that fantastic performance, and he was cool as a cucumber.

Since then, he has traveled the world, having amazing educational adventures, following his dream of becoming a marine biologist. And all of this he achieved quickly and easily without drugs or psychotherapy. He is aware that *he* made those changes in himself and that with his superpower *he* can make other changes in the future.

This kind of intervention is not practitioner-driven, but client-driven. When a client knows that *he* is the one making the change, not the practitioner, he gets a jolt of self-confidence that snowballs in a wonderful way. *I did that,* Jake acknowledged to himself. *I didn't think I'd ever be able to change that feeling, but I did, and it was so much easier than I thought it would be.* If he can do that, then he can do *this* ... and *this* ...

I call this *real control,* as opposed to the *illusory control* of discipline and willpower—those conscious, rational techniques in which someone actively *tries* to control their feelings, thoughts, and actions. From what I've seen, as soon as people *try* to take control of these things, they lose it. It may seem counterintuitive, but to get real control of our brains, we have to give up the fight. We have to listen to what resonates with us, what makes us *feel* good, and go with it, understanding that our brains are ultimately on a mission to protect us all the time and that—intending to be more successful next time—they will autocorrect any missteps or misjudgments. This autocorrection in response to prediction error, i.e., differences in what our brains predict will happen and what actually happens, is an unconscious process that can be tapped into, using unconsciously oriented brain hacks.

Sometimes the brain's survival mission gets out of hand, and we overreact. I've seen some crazy issues of this sort walk into my office over the years, like the client who was so afraid of dinosaurs that when, driving cross-country, she saw a life-size brontosaurus replica on the side of the road, she almost crashed a car full of her friends. A feeling so intense and out of control seems to the person experiencing it unthinkable to change. It is an activation of the sympathetic nervous system, which quickly makes us alert and energized to fight or flee from threats and dangers, whether merely perceived or real. Seeing the dinosaur set off that ancient distress signal, in response to which a surge of adrenaline and other stress hormones flooded her body. When this happens, we feel we are in a state of emergency.

Equally amazing, it's usually a one-session fix, using the right techniques—by simply capitalizing on how the brain works. I helped her eliminate the panicky body response to, in this case, a dinosaur, by experiencing a dinosaur, using mental imagery while feeling relaxed in the process. Consequently, her brain reconstructed its concept of "dinosaur" to no longer include that fight-or-flight survival response. She didn't enjoy seeing dinosaurs after that, but she didn't panic, either.

I, myself have experienced this phenomenon. For a short time, I had to take several long flights across the country in rapid succession, and during the last one I wound up in a really bad experience. I remember sitting in my seat, looking at the exit door, trying to figure out how I could get to it and open it so I could get out without anyone stopping me. We were a good thirty thousand feet up in the air, and what went through my mind was, *This is the dumbest thought I've ever had in my life.* Yet it was stronger than I was. I recognized all the signs of a fight-or-flight response. I was sweating and breathing really hard, and my heart was beating fast, like it would explode out of my chest.

From my psychology classes I understood that this was a panic attack and reminded myself it would quickly pass, that I just had to stay in my seat and hold it together for a few moments. I thought I was doing so well until the woman sitting next to me patted my hand and said, "It's okay, honey. It's going to be okay."

Apparently I'm not handling this as well as I thought I was, I told myself. But I got through it a few seconds later and knew I wouldn't be flying anywhere again anytime soon. Just thinking about flying after that made me feel a bit of that uncomfortable body response I'd experienced on the plane.

During my hypnotherapy training I was a guinea pig for our class to learn how to help people get rid of the fight-or-flight response that sometimes accompanies fear programming. After one session, about twenty minutes or so, which consisted of a combination of hypnosis, NLP, and imagery, I no longer felt that body response when I remembered that difficult plane ride. About an hour later I was standing, looking down from a very high bridge over a freeway without any fear whatsoever. A year later I seized the opportunity to go up in a hot air balloon that was tethered to the ground but went really far up. How would I feel? I wondered. Was I really cured? I was happy to go up in it and look over the side of the basket way down at the ground with no fear. It was so cool.

People feel helpless to control or have serious input over their life experiences all the time. For one reason or another, they just can't change how they think, feel, or behave. They are *blocked*. Optimistically they set the same goal on their New Year's resolution list year after year, or they might hesitate to engage in an activity, or they may think they're not good enough to try something they have a hunch they'd love. And their reliance on discipline or willpower to see them through falters, even fails them. This happens when they omit the importance of unconscious processes, which drive everything they do, think, and feel.

Considering that *very little* brain activity is consciously controlled (maybe 5 percent on a good day, likely limited to voluntary motor activity),[1] the unconscious is going to win every time the two are at odds. Since it was first proposed a century ago in the form of Émile Coué's *Law of Reversed Effort*, which states that if our conscious will is in conflict with fantasy, the fantasy will win, this idea has been non-controversial.[2] In fact, according to psychologist Karl Lashley,

"No activity of mind is ever conscious."[3] And from George Miller, "It is the result of thinking, not the process of thinking, that appears spontaneously in consciousness."[4]

"The conscious you, in effect, is like a not terribly bright CEO, whose subordinates do all of the research, draft all of the documents, then lay them out and say, 'Sign here, sir.' The CEO does—and takes the credit," writes Jeffrey Kluger in his *Time* article "Why You're Pretty Much Unconscious All the Time."

To neuroscientist Ezequiel Morsella, "The information we perceive in our consciousness is not created by conscious thought. Nor is it reacted to by conscious processes. Consciousness is the middleman and it doesn't do as much work as you think."[5] Further, if the programming is survival related, then to the person experiencing it, it may seem too strong to ever change. Therefore, they come to view it as just part of who they are and construct a life that accommodates that limitation. But this is a fallacy. Our lives don't have to include these limitations.

I see examples all the time where the unconscious has one agenda and the clients are exerting willpower to change it—berating themselves, talking harshly about their failure, and generally feeling like they're engaged in an internal war. From a survival-programming standpoint, one kind of issue that has always amazed me is the kids who won't eat, which seems as biologically counterproductive as you can get. Some unconscious fear even more powerful than survival drives them not to eat. Their terrified parents are frustrated because all the doctors they consulted said nothing was physically wrong. And psychotherapy wasn't helping these kids. Some come into my office crying because they have hit their breaking point and don't really know what I do or if I can help, but I'm their last resort.

One of my young clients would only drink chocolate milk. Another refused everything, even water. I remember the latter wriggling around in the big, comfy office recliner as I led him through a visual exercise to reprogram his feelings about eating and drinking, tapping into his brain's natural reconstruction processes.

My treatment must have looked to his parents like a complete sham. It was quick and easy. The scowl on his dad's face said to me, "This is the biggest waste of money ever." Happily, not only was my client eating and drinking just after that, but the parents returned for sessions to free up their blocks too. And the boy who would only drink chocolate milk? On the way home he asked his mom if they could stop for pizza. The next morning she sent me a heartfelt thank-you email.

Procrastination is perhaps the most common way that our brains block us. Whatever we say we want to do but actually don't do, or perhaps we put it off for a prolonged period of time, is either something that causes us stress or something we don't really want to do for whatever reason. Typically, it can be remedied by switching out the feeling associated with that task; that is, by unconsciously reconstructing the neural connections to put a good or neutral feeling in place of the bad feeling—thereby lowering the stress level we hit when we think about doing it. Other times it may be more complicated, and the person needs to investigate why he balks at making that decision. *What is holding me back?* The correct information is unconscious, though; rational thought will not reveal it. He cannot "think the answer" into his awareness.

Sometimes unconscious survival programming is so extreme that it alters memories or makes them inaccessible. This unconscious process of forgetting emotionally difficult memories, which the esteemed French philosopher Pierre Janet, considered one of the fathers of psychology, termed *dissociation,* is a way that our brains naturally protect us. Pierre came upon this idea from the following interesting conundrum brought forth by his uncle Paul.

In 1884, the eminent French philosopher Paul Janet (1823–'99) introduced the problem of posthypnotic suggestion. A hypnotized subject is given the posthypnotic command to return to the hypnotist in thirteen days. Awake, the subject seems never to remember the command yet nonetheless fulfils it. The problem then is this: how does the subject count thirteen days without knowing it? Two years later, the philosopher and psychologist Pierre Janet (1859–'47) would submit the concept of dissociation as a solution to his uncle's query. He proposed that a second consciousness kept track of time and executed the suggestion outside the awareness of the main consciousness. His solution also provided a psychological framework for describing multiple personality, hysteria, and spirit possession. It led to the first purely psychological conceptualization of traumatic memory, which then furnished Sigmund Freud with a theoretical base upon which to build his theory of psychoanalysis.[6]

Dissociation, a form of emotional distancing, is often seen in people who have had traumatic experiences, especially when they were little. Telling themselves they don't feel bad doesn't work, *so their brains hide the memories* in some mental closet, allowing them to go about their days without being overcome by, or falling apart at the mere presence of, those bad feelings. While this is a good short-term strategy for getting on with one's life after intense emotional pain, it is far from a good long-term strategy, as the memories in those closets continue to impact us in ways we can't control and probably don't like. And the longer we keep them hidden, the more problems they may cause.

It's like the unconscious tries to tell us we need to get rid of that emotional toxicity by making us overreact sometimes or giving us a stomachache or an allergy attack. If we don't do something to get rid of the bad feelings from that locked-up memory, the brain will up the ante and give us some other issue. "Are you listening now?" If we still don't get rid of it, our brain will pile on yet another difficulty. It will do this to try to get our attention so we let go of that monster in the closet. But first, we have to see it. Just like the rest of the body, the brain defaults toward health.

One difficult hidden emotional experience can eventually cause multiple issues. Like with my young client who was afraid of flying, that fear generalized to high places and was making crowds a problem too. Some prospective clients come in with a list of issues they want to be free from, and I tell them to choose a single superficial one to start with—for example, a fear of flying rather than increased self-worth. As they change their feelings about the superficial issue, we'll follow the brain back to more deeply recessed and self-referential issues, priming the pump for deeper causes. And as they reprogram, or reconstruct, those neurological representations of those feelings, more and more items fall off their list. That single, deep core cause, such as a buried feeling of not being good enough, can, over the years, manifest as disparate psychological and physical problems.

That's not to say that all issues come from a single, deep personal issue. Many superficial issues are just that, superficial. Because we may be able to handle them, those may actually be more likely to keep us from getting help to snuff them out. Sometimes we can tell ourselves to cowgirl up and push through any difficulty to reach a goal. Or maybe all we need is a little support from others to light a fire in us to get us to the finish line. Perhaps adding structure to our day, blocking out time to get everything done, enables us to have the personal time we really want at the end of a workday. When these strategies work, they can increase our confidence and reconstruct our mental concepts for these activities, increasing the probability that they'll get easier and make us feel better and better.

All too often, though, rational, conscious techniques like these only get us just so far, as with my polygraph test. They may fail outright, fail eventually, or at the very least increase the energy we need to put into them as we force our way through, leaving less energy for anything else, like having a life or getting more work done or coming up with innovative ideas.

Before seeing me, many of my future clients used self-help books or programs, or they attended live events with gurus they expected to get them past their blocks. They joined support groups, built up excitement, and posted sticky notes full of positive affirmations all over their bathroom mirrors. But they came up with a plan to move forward, only to have it fall flat shortly after starting. When they arrived to consult with me, they inevitably expressed that they felt broken—something was wrong with them—because their failure couldn't possibly be the guru's fault. The limiting beliefs they started with strengthened, and they felt disempowered.

For most people, the next step is to consult a doctor or psychotherapist. A doctor may prescribe medication, such as an antianxiety drug. Sometimes this helps. Sometimes not. A psychotherapist can help someone understand their issue or provide a coping strategy. As with medication, therapy can be very useful. Some people, however, such as the ones who come to me for help, are largely the ones who found medication and/or therapy to be of limited usefulness for them or they just don't resonate with those options.

I've had clients book sessions with me shortly after therapy sessions because they felt bad after those sessions but felt good after ours. Conversely, some people don't have success with unconscious strategies like the ones I use, and for them medication and/or traditional therapy may be what they need. Often I find that combining what I do with other strategies that doctors and/or psychotherapists offer can be a really effective one-two punch to help people get on a better track and live the lives they want.

The best approach to eliminating discomfort depends, of course, on the cause. Physical causes require mechanical or chemical solutions, and psychological causes require mental reconstruction. Unfortunately, the cause is not always obvious. Often doctors will not be able to tell their patients what is causing a problem, so they prescribe medications not to cure them but to help them feel more at ease. Such treatment is a Band-Aid, or coping strategy, that might be offered by a therapist or coach. In those cases an unconsciously oriented strategy may be more effective by allowing the client to actually root out the cause of the problem.

Sometimes even when there is a physical problem, there may not be a physical solution. One of my clients, a doctor, had intractable pain. He had been to all relevant medical specialists, who determined that he had an abnormality in the tissue that covered his brain, but there was nothing they could do about it. Having dealt with the issue at length, he'd developed anger issues and even suicidal ideation from self-imposed isolation from family and friends due to this physical and emotional discomfort. After one session to reduce physical discomfort and stress, he felt less pain and less anger, and his suicidal thoughts vanished.

With some psychotherapy patients I see the same thing. For example, I had a prospective client want to see how hypnotherapy would work for him, and just prior to his first session I received a call from his counselor to discuss his case. She wanted to start EMDR (eye movement desensitization and reprocessing) therapy with him but felt he was too stressed out for it. She wanted to know what I would be doing with him. When I told her my work would be to reduce his stress level, she was elated. If I could help him reduce his arousal enough, she could introduce EMDR to him, she said.

Then came his first session with me. It just took one. After that, he was calm enough to start EMDR with her. From then on, she sent stressed-out clients to me to prepare them for working with her.

Another client wanted to try EMDR with her psychotherapist for past trauma but was told she could not start using that technique until she got rid of the daily flashbacks she suffered related to a traumatic experience. After one unconsciously oriented session her flashbacks were gone. And her therapist discovered she did not need EMDR at all.

To their patients for whom there is no effective physical cure or for whom therapy could be problematic, some doctors and therapists are quick to recommend more unconscious strategies. Too many others, unfortunately, do not see such interventions as viable alternatives and therefore do not even let their patients know they exist. Despite the wealth of anecdotal and empirical evidence supporting its effectiveness, misinformation abounds. In the general population, based in disapproval by doctors, therapists, and coaches, as well as misinformation spread by movies and television shows and even spiritual leaders, there is mistrust and even fear of these techniques. More than one client has come to me, worried about starting sessions because their church leader told them that it opened the mind to let the devil in.

Even educated people have a fear of using unconscious-oriented interventions to help them past their blocks. My very first client was so desperate to try hypnotherapy for what she described as a self-generated limit on how much money she could make that she didn't even care that my recliner hadn't been delivered to my office, yet. Even so, to try hypnotherapy scared her. I asked why, and she recounted how her son was chosen to go up on the stage in a show using hypnosis for entertainment. He was hypnotized, but the hypnotist was unable to wake him. I asked her if the hypnotist explained why, and she said that he did not. I asked if her son was a workaholic, by chance, and she said he was. I told her that he was probably more deeply relaxed than he had been in a while and he just wanted to stay there for a bit longer. Her son, I explained, was in complete control of whether he was under hypnosis or not and what he did or did not do, and that in her sessions she would be in complete control, as well. We went on to do some great work together.

Unconscious strategies like hypnotherapy can be amazingly fast and effective at helping release blocks to growth and wellbeing. Understanding why these blocks occur in the first place can help us understand how these strategies can work with our natural brain processes to mitigate these impediments.

Chapter Two

Birth of a Block

WE SEE UNCONSCIOUS BLOCKS manifest in many different ways. From sleep disturbances to an apparent lack of emotional control, our brains let us know—beneath our awareness—when there's an issue that our brains, for some reason of their own, have decided needs to be addressed. Just because we are not consciously aware of the issue does not mean it's not impacting us.

Anything that really bothers us will pop up at some point from our unconscious minds into our awareness, perhaps as overreactions, like having a complete freak-out about something that really isn't a big deal; for example, a woman who was so stressed out because her husband routinely dropped his dirty socks on the floor next to the dirty laundry basket rather than putting them in the basket. But her intense reaction did not come from that careless action itself; her brain associated it with a more intense emotional event. We also see unresolved emotional difficulties in conversations—for instance, the non sequitur made by a client when talking about her early childhood; in the middle of her story she casually slipped in the comment that her father had sexually assaulted her when she was two years old, after which she continued her more benign story as if not having said anything alarming.

Avoiding situations can indicate blocks, as well. Someone who will take really slow, winding back roads for the sole purpose of avoiding driving on freeways, which she finds intensely frightening, is painfully aware she has a block it would be great to get rid of. Determining what jobs you take based on whether you'll have to give a presentation in front of people also indicates a block. Have to leave the house when someone's watching a show about war on the television because it makes you very sad or angry or upset? There's your sign.

But aha moments also pop up from our unconscious minds. After we've been trying to solve a problem for a while, we can get to the point of giving up, focus on something else, but our unconscious processes keep running. When our brain devises a solution that resonates with us or makes us feel comfortable, it appears in our conscious minds as if from nowhere. One of my clients had been really wracking her brain to figure out what to do about her difficult son, then one day woke from a nap with the answer fully formed. She instantly knew it was right because thinking about it made her feel relaxed and peaceful.

In problem-solving, we engage our creative thought processes, which are unconsciously driven. Steve Jobs, one of the founders of Apple, once said, "Creativity is just connecting things. When you ask creative people how they did something, they feel a little guilty because they didn't really do it, they just saw something. It seemed obvious to them after a while."[7]

And let's not forget that special level of hell in which we're almost asleep (in a hypnogogic state) and our brain picks that time to ask why we park on driveways but drive on parkways. At last asleep, perhaps we have a recurring dream or variations on a theme. It's as if the unconscious mind is trying to tell us something, but what? When a client and I focus on a recurring dream in my office, the client can finally hear what her mind has been trying to tell her and make whatever changes she feels appropriate, putting an end to that nagging issue.

Often, whatever you don't work out during the day, your brain tries to work out at night while you sleep or whenever you slip into that hypnotic state in which your unconscious mind is running the show. That state enables you to change brain programs that aren't serving you, because that's when the right hemisphere of the brain is in charge. Allowing that part of the brain to be in control, you can understand and change maladaptive thoughts, feelings, and behaviors and do more of what serves you—what resonates with who you really are at your core, your self-concept. That to me is real control. You know it's correct because afterwards you no longer experience the same overreactions or other unconscious negative influences.

Blocks can come from simple or complex causes. Consider a fear of snakes. One client developed her fear after almost stepping on a rattlesnake in a hike in the desert; it scared the hell out of her, and she froze. This obviously natural fear, though constructive for survival, in her case ran haywire. One day looking at her phone, she saw a picture of a snake posted by a friend on social media. Instantly, she threw her phone across the room. Figuring she ought to get a handle on that, she came in for a session. After that first session, in which we deleted the fight-or-flight response from her mental concept of snakes, she texted me from the pet shop down the street from my office: "Guess where I am now?!!" accompanied by a photo of the snake tank right in front of her. No longer did she fear snakes.

Contrast that case with another client—this one terrorized by her younger sister when she was growing up. Her sister loved torturing her by dangling snakes in front of her and leaving them places—like under her pillow—for her to discover, finding it amusing to see her freak out. Her fear of snakes was complicated by other uncomfortable feelings and limiting beliefs, such as a sense of unworthiness, trust issues, etc., that accompanied mean behavior by a sister who should have shown her love and protection. To get rid of her fear of snakes required about six sessions because we had to help the brain deal with those other issues in the fallout.

We don't always have to know where blocks originate. For thirty years one of my clients endured a condition called globus, in which he felt there was something stuck in his throat when nothing was actually there. Often sensations like this come from a traumatic event, such as actually having had something stuck in his throat and feeling the fear of choking to death. This client, however, couldn't remember anything like that ever happening (but it was possible a very long time ago, he conceded). All he knew was that almost all the time he was uncomfortable, and he had difficulty sleeping and living a relaxed, happy life because of it.

He went to every doctor he could find and tried an assortment of therapies. Nothing worked. Having used hypnotherapy successfully to quit smoking, he wondered: *Might it work for my globus?*

It took just one session to get rid of that feeling. I gave him some self-hypnosis homework and asked him to let me know how it went. Three weeks later he contacted me with the news that he kept waiting for that sensation to return but it hadn't. If it did, he would let me know. But as it was, he just wanted to thank me for finally ridding him of that affliction. I never heard from him again.

As mentioned in the previous chapter, it's not that uncommon for a prospective client to come into a consultation with a list of issues to fix, all of which are blocking him from living the life he wants to live. Those lists can be quite long and sprinkled with superficial issues. The inclusion of deeper, more self-referential issues, such as a lack of confidence or self-esteem, on the list strongly hints at more complex causes behind even the most superficial of problems. In that case, we start with a rather surface-level issue to focus on first, such as letting go of a fear or a coping behavior like smoking. When we get rid of that, we prime the brain to let us know more about what past events might have contributed to the cause. We reprogram any negative emotion, physical discomfort, and/or limiting beliefs the brain had included in its construction of that memory, then let the brain lead us to the next, usually more impactful, event that needs to be reconstructed to completely get rid of the issue.

Following this protocol, I typically see the brain utilize a stepping-stone kind of process to completely reprogram an issue. After the client makes a change in the superficial manifestation of the issue (e.g., fear, smoking), it's as if we opened an unconscious mental closet in which the brain has locked some monsters, what Pierre Janet termed the *subconscious* mind, which is our go-to short-term coping mechanism for dealing with (or not) difficult events. We are a social species, and nobody wants to be around us if we are hung up on something our dad said to us when we were five, so we lock it in the monster closet. Our brains are really good at clearing unhealthy emotions, but sometimes they have trouble and just bury something emotionally toxic in the monster closet. That's what unconsciously oriented tools are really helpful in dealing with: they give the brain a helping hand to open that closet and completely release those emotional monsters.

Letting the unconscious brain processes lead us to their monsters of choice, we first see them pick out a little monster, perhaps to test the waters, as—intuitively speaking—one would expect there to be apprehension about letting any monsters out of the closet. The brain put them there for a reason: because they were difficult to handle. *Is the client, as determined by unconscious selection and filtering mechanisms, strong enough to handle them now?* Hypnosis helps to open those doors by keeping the client feeling comfortable and supported enough to take that brave step.

Hypnosis also reduces arousal so that it doesn't go too high once the closet is opened. In a conscious state, that increased baseline arousal may make it too stressful to face the monsters inside, so the brain prevents that from happening. It's always protecting us, even from ourselves.

I've seen an interesting phenomenon occur when clients try to face a monster too soon. The brain will have a freak-out. The first time I saw this was with a client who knew what memory we were going to work with but could not visualize anything when she tried to see it. All she saw was "a black veil." Even moving her head from side to side in the recliner, she couldn't see around it.

Another client ran into exactly the same thing: he was trying to work on a recent, very painful traumatic memory, and a "black veil" obscured his vision. After this second appearance of a black veil, I felt it premature for my clients to go straight for the big monsters. Using a more organic method, I let the unconscious part of the brain bring up what it wants to work on—as big a monster as it is comfortable confronting. I encourage my clients to stop directing their brains and just be open to what comes up, instead. Since adopting that strategy a decade ago I have not been stymied by "the black veil."

Both of these clients had remarkable visualization abilities—nothing lacking there. So what was going on? The brain, in its wisdom, may simply have been exercising sensible protection. Evolution 101. If the brain deems a thought, feeling, or action too risky emotionally or physically, it will stop us from engaging in it. The black veil kept my clients from visualizing an event that their brains, it would appear, decided could not yet be processed successfully.

In both cases, working with the client for just a few minutes—letting the brain naturally decide what to bring up to remove the black veil—I helped them release the fear that kept the brain in protective mode. And—bam! Immediately a rich, detailed, colorful tableau appeared in front of them, so they could now rid themselves of that big monster.

Once that smallest monster that was deemed difficult enough or uncomfortable enough to lock in the closet is out—and much easier to get rid of than the client expected—the client gets a shot of confidence, feeling empowered, which makes it simpler to deal with a more fearful threat next time. At some point, the brain finds its way back to the biggest, baddest monster, which we call the *initial sensitizing event* (ISE), from which the issue was created and all of its manifestations developed.

The ISE often occurs early in life. Into our thirties, our brains are still developing, so emotionally difficult events before that development is complete will result in, usually, half-baked solutions. It is easy to understand how a young brain would be inclined to put such events into a closet, because the mental machinery is typically not fine-tuned enough to effectively resolve them.

I had a client who had suffered from a litany of autoimmune illnesses throughout most of her sixty years. When I met her, she suffered from a debilitating eye condition, even with medication. She described vivid dreams, which were always incredibly interesting to hear about, as they revealed wonderful clues to the motives of her mind. In one such dream she carefully wrapped up all her internal organs in white butcher paper and lovingly put them back into her body. If that doesn't say "protection," I don't know what does.

Physically she felt better as we followed her brain into the closet and started banishing monsters. And her doctor took her off her medication. Then she visited her family, had an outbreak again, and reverted to her meds. Finally, after that, she was willing to address some long-avoided family issues. She told me she was sexually molested by her uncle when she was five. Her mother, when the little girl informed her about the situation, encouraged her to go sit on the uncle's lap and give him a kiss.

She remembered the exact moment, at *five years old*, when she decided that she was now an adult so that she could protect herself, because no adult was protecting her and she couldn't protect herself as a child. That programming likely served her at that time but eventually became maladaptive. Once she successfully addressed that ISE in our sessions, reconstructing her self-concept to include being able now to take care of herself, her uveitis vanished, and her doctor took her off of her medication for good.

She also got a new condo that she had denied herself for years, and she restructured her business so that she worked when she wanted to and had time off when she wanted. Her friend who referred her to me in the first place told me she couldn't believe she was the same person;

"I want whatever you're giving her!" she said. The entire process took twelve sessions.

Life improvements like these are awesome ramifications of pulling the weeds out by the roots rather than simply changing superficial behaviors we don't want. People start creating the lives they really want to live. Career changes are common, as they see the limitations of where they've kept themselves professionally and start to feel deserving of getting more out of life. They start putting up healthy boundaries with others and do more of what makes them happy.

Successfully reprogramming one ISE often results in many issues being left by the wayside, as explained earlier. It's as if the brain tries to draw attention to the issue by making the client feel bad, revealing in this way that the issue was relegated to the monster closet instead of being processed and released. It keeps impacting the client, though, so at some point the brain lets the person know it's time to deal with it. This communication is nonverbal, below the surface of consciousness, so the person may start feeling cranky in a given situation that is associated with that issue in his memory.

If he doesn't take the hint and do something about getting rid of that monster, then his brain will change the stakes, as I mentioned previously: "Let's give him migraines," the brain appears to say. "Are you listening now?" If he starts taking migraine medication instead of seeing that discomfort as an indicator of a monster that the brain wants to release, then his brain might respond with fits of anger, or allergies, or untenable anxiety, as if to say: "Are you listening *now*?"

It's amazing how many problems, both psychological and physical, simply vanish after an emotional monster is banished from the unconscious closet in which it had been imprisoned for years or even decades. And when that happens, when the client releases that emotional weight that she had been suffering under all that time, she feels noticeably physically lighter. Upon releasing emotional fallout from an ISE when she was two years old, one of my elderly clients kept looking down at her stomach.

"What are you looking at?" I asked.

"I feel twenty pounds lighter!"

It's the best feeling ever. If I could bottle that feeling, I could retire early.

Chapter Three

How the Brain Works

———◆O◆———

A DIFFERENT FEELING OF lightness filled me in the village of Giverny, France, even though it was dark and drizzling. As our bus passed through the little town on our way from Vernon to Auvers-Sur-Oise and the resting place of Vincent Van Gogh, I instantly recognized the subjects of many paintings by my all-time-favorite artist, Claude Monet. On the left of the bus was his small garden with an archway of beautiful flowers; to the right was the pond where he created his famous waterlily paintings. I had been a bit disappointed that the exhibit of those paintings at the Musée de l'Orangerie in Paris was not on our scheduled stops, but the very brief glimpses of the gardens, pond, and even the field where he painted boring haystacks in a way that make the soul sing was so much more intriguing. It was a spiritual experience for me, the effects of which will last my entire life, much longer than the several seconds it took the bus to pass by in the rain.

My awareness changed. Concepts changed. I've always heard that there are no boring subjects, just boring painters. I used to try to seek out interesting subjects to paint, but now I'll find intriguing ways to paint any subjects. My concept of what it means to express myself in paint has changed fundamentally, and I will never be able to look at a Monet without seeing the genius of his work. Choosing an "interesting" subject means I have limiting beliefs about myself as an artist. That stops now.

Those few seconds changed the information in my consciousness in a way that I can never un-see it. As I look out the rain-spattered windows of my cruise ship that is docked in Rouen, I cannot help but view the mundane sights around me as changes in value, of dark and light, and see the colors I could use to paint these scenes in terms of value more than hue, as the artist who gave us an Impressionist watercolor workshop the other day taught us to do. I see the world differently now, and I cannot go back to seeing it the way I used to. There's a feeling of awe as I peer out the windows now that wasn't there before. It is generated unconsciously, allowing different information to reach my conscious mind now. I begin to wonder what is real—the drab scene I see in front of me or the more colorful emotional experience of that same view that the artist in me (or anyone) could share in a way that differs from the information that's coming up to my brain through my eyes. As my awareness shifts and I paint, I change the way other brains unconsciously process information. That, for me, is the purpose of making art.

There is no universally agreed-upon definition or concept of consciousness, other than generally equating it with awareness. In fact, it's in a gray area between science and philosophy. Are humans entirely physical? Or a spirit, a soul, beyond the physical? What's the relationship between brains and consciousness, between the stuff in our skulls and the experience in our minds? We are aware of very little of our brain activity, and the thoughts and feelings that we are conscious of are created by unconscious brain processes. At some unconscious level, selection and filtering mechanisms shuttle some information to the conscious mind, into our awareness. But that's just a tiny amount of the entirety of information in the brain, the teeny-tiny tip of an enormous iceberg.

The mind and body are two sides of the same coin; what affects one affects the other. But how the brain conjures conscious awareness from the electrical activity of billions of individual nerve cells remains one of the great unanswered questions of life. For the purposes of my work and this book, if we can intentionally focus our attention on it, it is conscious.

As we focus our attention, "attending" to what's going around us or on what's going on inside of us, this attentional focus is like a flashlight we can move unconsciously or intentionally (consciously), using the information to determine if there is anything in it that might be important to us; if so, then we can focus on that. In this way, we can detect any threats to our safety present in our surroundings; also, whether there is anything that can increase our probability of surviving or thriving. This input feeds into a control network in our brains that modulates our actions in light of what we need more or less of to live successfully. This type of homeostasis—or dynamic equilibrium—is called our *body budget*, and our brains are constantly modifying our activity to try to keep our body budget in a healthy place. Our body, like our finances, needs its budget to stay healthy.

Intriguingly, that sensory information that comes into our brains from our eyes, ears, and other sense organs works in a counterintuitive way. Unless you know quite a bit about vision, you might think that when you look at an object, the visual information stimulates photoreceptors in your eyes, and that stimulation pattern travels to the brain *as visual information* for you to analyze. Then you can decide what to do about it.

This is what we call a *bottom-up* neural process. It goes like this: Cells in our nervous system, called *neurons*, electrochemically move information from our eyes to our brains' lower-level visual processing centers for identification, starting with lines and moving up to patterns and then objects. Then that information informs higher levels of brain processing that enable us to understand what to make of what we see and what to do about it.

True, there are neural connections that indeed support this sequence of events; however, those connections are heavily influenced by *top-down* connections.

In fact, only one-tenth of the connections between our eyes and our brains shuttle information upwards. The other 90 percent goes down. The higher-level brain areas that deal with our understanding, feelings, beliefs, etc., in fact, *modify* the information coming up from our eyes and allow the brain to predict what we will see. Our brains run on unconscious prediction, not conscious stimulation.

Because of the way the nervous system works, therefore, we do not believe what we see; *we see what we believe*. Your brain's prior beliefs—prejudices, perspectives—inform what you think you see. This is true for all of us. It's not by sensory input, but by higher-level prediction, that our interaction with the world is initiated.

There are almost a hundred billion neurons in our brains, interconnected in complex and meaningful ways. They help us make sense of the world. Those connections allow us to construct our reality, to predict and control our thoughts, feelings, and actions. But that reality is constantly being reconstructed by feedback we get during our interactions with the world. When our predictions about our upcoming interactions with the world fall short, creating *prediction error*, as mentioned in Chapter One, our brains automatically make corrections to improve our future interactions.

We don't have to try to have a better interaction next time. Because automatic fine-tuning is constantly being done, *the correct program will run even better next time*. In fact, consciously trying to change how we react in a given situation often makes us perform worse. This is because our conscious minds are only aware of and able to process a very small amount of information at any given time, and only in a serial way: one idea follows another. But while we are consciously processing information serially, *the overwhelming amount of our brain activity is parallel; it all happens at once*. If we had the ability to be conscious of every bit of this activity, it would completely overwhelm and paralyze us. After all, the human brain has been described as the most complex known structure in the universe.[8]

Our brains use information from words, nonverbal behaviors, our senses, our external modes of communication, and many other sources to make automatic changes in our concepts, but our conscious minds only pick up a few of them and one at a time. That's why I say unconscious brain activity is parallel. It's processing everything it knows about a topic—all at once.

Conflict results when we consciously try to modify or control our interactions rather than relying on our unconscious body-budget modifications to guide us. This may sound heretical, recommending that we just relinquish control. But it works. To get real control, we have to give it up.

I've had many high-level athletes in my office trying to get past a performance ceiling to go to the next level in their respective sports. One golfer, at a particular point in his swing, needed to shift his visual attention to a different area on the ball. A pickleball player needed to stop thinking about having a backup serve available if his power serve failed. The details differ, but the athletes all had one thing in common: they needed to stop their conscious minds from interfering in the highly practiced and finely honed sensorimotor processes that are engaged when playing their sports. In other words, after practicing hard, just let go. Performers call this being in that proverbial "zone," or "flow state."

We see this in daily life too. If we try to *control* a response instead of letting our brain and body operate on automatic pilot, we don't do as well. You might be performing some activity, like sorting papers, really well. But just start thinking about it; right away, you mess up. Especially during tasks that don't require a lot of thought, the conscious mind can really get in our way. And it really gets in our way when it comes to responses that need to be fast. When you encounter a bear, you have to act quickly; there's no time to send anything to committee.

All of this is to say that we have neural circuits in our brains whose job it is to construct memories,[9] emotions,[10] pain and all other forms of perception, the self, concept development, brain development—in other words, construction and reconstruction with respect to body budget is how the brain works. This reconstruction depends on a type of *neuroplasticity*, a concept that was ruled out for centuries, until research in the late 1960s and afterwards proved that adult brains can change, building new pathways and modifying established ones to increase the probability of implementing certain concepts and responses that serve us better.

Though the processes implicated in neuroplasticity are unconscious, we can be consciously aware of the results. Sometimes we consciously know that something we did wasn't well received and that for sure we'll be doing it differently next time. We're aware of some of the revisions we'll make, but for the most part, what will happen is unconscious reconstruction of the relevant concepts. When we have a negative interaction with the world, that interaction affects us through a lesser-known sense we possess called *interoception*, which gives us feedback by way of changes in heart rate, blood pressure, etc.

These interoceptive changes are concerned with *arousal* (commonly referred to as stress) and *affect* (commonly referred to as emotion). Just as with the level of sugar in our blood or the pH of our tissues, there is an optimal range within which our brain, in concert with the rest of our body, works to keep our arousal—our stress level—not too high or too low. Too high, and we implode. Too low, and we are comatose. There's a happy medium. This idea is not new; in fact, the Yerkes-Dodson law of optimal arousal for optimal performance has been around for over a century. During that time, this optimal-range idea has been used to explain other behavioral and cognitive activities, as well. Optimal arousal, given the task or situation, is an important part of balancing our body budget.

The other part of interoception is affect, or emotion, which comes mainly from prediction. For many years, research supported the idea that our distinct, universal emotions correspond to distinct, universal expressions. If you see someone you've never met, who may live anywhere in the world, smile, you know that person is happy, right? You don't have to know their culture to understand what that smile means—or so we've thought until recently.

In the past, researchers spent an amazing amount of time and effort in categorizing different emotions. They even identified distinctions among primary emotions, secondary emotions (which arise from combining primary emotions), and even tertiary emotions. Do all people really come hardwired for all of these different emotions? Newer, more advanced research says no, we do not; rather, we construct emotional concepts using interoceptive information during early social interactions in which an emotion such as happiness is displayed and named by those around us. That is, it's a learned response. This makes a lot of sense when you think about it. Do you really know what a stranger's smile means? Perhaps she isn't happy at all but putting on a smile so you think she is and won't ask any questions she doesn't want to answer. Distinct emotions are not innate; they are constructed and then reconstructed in light of prediction error.

We know that our mental concepts are changing all the time, with additional experience. In interacting with our world, we come to realize that a frown doesn't necessarily mean someone is sad. We construct and reconstruct our interpretations. If you're feeling aroused and you're on a swaying suspension bridge, you must be afraid. By contrast, if you're aroused while talking to a woman, you must be excited because you find her attractive.[11]

It used to be thought that when we aren't actively participating in a task, our brains are quiet and at rest. Now we know that during these down times, there is increased activity in what is called the Default Mode Network (DMN), which forms neural interconnections among several parts of the brain. So even at "rest" our brains are doing something. DMN activity increases when we turn our attention inward (as in hypnosis or meditation), when we relate to and empathize with a friend's situation, when we focus on our memories, and when we dream about the future.[12]

DMN activity sometimes tells us what we need, which drives motivation. Its activation increases drug craving and withdrawal and tends to be suppressed with substance use.[13] The Default Mode Network may be instrumental in both blocking us (by misdirected motivation or a lack of motivation) and clearing such blocks. Sometimes we feel we need one thing, when—as in the story of the smoker at the beginning of the book—it is actually a conscious misperception of a deeper need we're trying to fill.

One day a lovely older woman came into my office, intent on losing weight. Every day she felt the need to stop in at her local bakery on her way home from work. The urge was irresistible. She had to stop there for a cupcake. Every day. She realized she had a problem when her grandson started calling her "Cookie Monster." After one session she no longer wanted any sweets or alcohol, and she no longer felt like stopping by the bakery. It no longer interested her. She also noticed, though, that her sleep had taken a turn for the worse. In our next session we investigated the source of the sleep disturbance and found that she hadn't been happy since moving to Arizona several years prior; she dearly missed her close circle of friends left behind.

Her need for being "home" in California was temporarily assuaged by eating a cupcake, but that cupcake high was short-lived and didn't actually fill the gaping need. Her body didn't crave a cupcake; in fact, that cupcake threw her body budget out of whack, just like smoking and other objects of abuse do. It just made her feel happy for a little while but masked the underlying problem. When she suddenly stopped eating cupcakes, her brain went into a freak-out from losing its coping strategy, and this frustration led to her sleep disturbance. She decided to move back home to California, and she has been there ever since, happy, free of her cupcake habit, and sleeping well.

Using unconscious strategies to tap into DMN activity can enlighten us about the real causes behind our maladaptive thoughts, feelings, and behaviors. Turning our attention inward, we listen to what those unconscious processes are trying to tell us that otherwise get lost in translation to our rational, conscious mind. When we stop trying to consciously direct how we feel and listen instead, we can reprogram the memories and reconstruct the relevant concepts, producing a change we may not have been able to make consciously.

The trick is to reconstruct memories and concepts in a way that excludes self-referential information. I see this all the time after even the most superficial of sessions. At the beginning of the session, clients describe unpleasant past events from a first-person perspective. After tapping into the unconscious to immediately reconstruct that memory without the negative emotion, they see the event from a third-person perspective. The self-referential part of the memory is gone; consequently, clients report that the event feels unimportant, like they're watching someone else—it could be anyone—in that situation, just not themselves. They also invariably report that the memory is more distant, isn't as clear, like it's foggy or behind cloudy glass, no longer in color, and without as much detail. Arousal is reduced, and their affect changes from negative to neutral or, in some cases, positive.

In rare cases the memory may completely disappear, as happened with a client I'll call John, who had an intractable anger issue. Under hypnosis his unconscious mind led us to a memory when he was a kid. His father, in the military, was very strict with him and his brother. They had to keep their room clean and tidy at all times. One day his brother left dirty clothes on the floor, and their father came home. The brother shoved the clothes under John's bed, not to get in trouble. But their father, misreading the situation, punished John severely—by destroying his collection of model airplanes, which John had spent many hours constructing and in which he took great pride. John was devastated. He described that memory to me in great detail, but after coming out of hypnosis, he had no memory of the event at all. Meanwhile, the anger subsided. He had met his objective in coming to me.

Do we remember things for future reference to improve our interactions with the world and have fewer difficulties? Deleting the emotion from John's traumatic childhood memory resulted in his brain deleting the entire memory. For some reason, the emotional reaction was the reason for holding on to it as long as he did. With the emotion gone, he had no further reason to keep the memory. I felt—and his brain evidently did as well—he had no more use for it. It could no longer negatively impact John's life. Regardless, in this case the reconstruction was a rearrangement of neural connections in such a way that the memory no longer existed in John's brain. Deleting it impacted John's body balance positively, that happy homeostasis that drives brain function.

So how do we open ourselves up to all of this rich information that we have in our heads to know what changes to make to balance our body budget? And how do we empower ourselves to do so? By inhibiting the natural filtering and selection of information we do when consciously trying to direct our thinking. Instead, we have to relax and let our minds flow.

Sigmund Freud developed a technique he called *free association*. You may be familiar with this concept. You think of one thing and let your mind bring up whatever is associated with it in your brain. This technique was arguably a form of hypnosis, though Freud would disagree because there was no formality of helping the person into a hypnotic state, which we call an induction. Free association opens the door to unconscious information processing, as do other everyday trance states. You put yourself into hypnosis often, when you're engrossed in a good book or driving (yes, "highway hypnosis" is actually a hypnotic state). If you're focusing on something and you don't hear your name being called or lose track of time and miss lunch, you're in a hypnotic, or trance, state. Free association allows the patient to direct what thoughts become consciously accessible rather than the therapist providing suggestions, as was the case with Josef Breuer's hypnosis method (developed in 1881 to 1882) upon which free association was based.

With his patient Anna O., Breuer attempted to get her to remember a trauma that was causing a symptom, on the theory that the memory would "eliminate the associated pathogenic memory through 'catharsis.'"

It was probably in August 1881 that the method acquired its definitive form. This was when Anna O., after refusing to drink water and suffering near-hydrophobia during hot weather, remembered the disgust she felt the moment she happened upon her English lady-companion's dog while it was drinking from a water glass. As soon as she described the event, she asked for water, and "thereupon the disturbance vanished, never to return." Other examples provided Breuer with evidence that "in the case of this patient the hysterical phenomena disappeared as soon as the event which had given rise to them was reproduced in her hypnosis," and that systematic application of what she called "chimney sweeping" put an end to one after another of such morbid phenomena. To move the treatment along faster, Breuer began regular use of hypnosis, which he had not previously.[14]

More recently, neuroscientist and neurophysicist Nancy Andreasen has researched brain activity when inducing what she refers to as "random episodic silent thought" (or REST), during which relaxed participants let their minds wander in free association. She tested their reactions, using positron emission tomography (PET) images. These scans showed great activity in the free-association areas of all participants when they were in the REST state, and those participants she designated as exceptionally creative (award-winning writers, scientists, etc.) showed even greater activity in these free-association areas.

So, well over a century later, we're still discussing free association in terms of a client-directed hypnotic state, whatever wording anyone wishes to use to label that, which allows us to access and process hidden information, making new and richer associations and coming up with ideas and solutions.

We often forget that the brain is part of the body, and that to make mental changes is to make changes in brain biochemistry and structure. Further, the brain is constantly interacting with the rest of the body, so mental changes can result in physical changes. We can demonstrate this with a simple activity. Close your eyes and imagine taking a big bite of a juicy lemon. Just writing those words made my mouth water! What caused that physical change? A mental activity. The implications of this idea are vast and explain the enormous percentage of visits to physicians that are chalked up to psychosomatic causes. A psychosomatic issue is a real physical problem whose cause is psychological, not physical. For such issues, physical interventions, such as medication, cannot cure the patient, though they may make them more comfortable temporarily as symptoms are relieved.

A mental cause of a physical problem requires a mental solution. Activating the Default Mode Network, or DMN, for inner reflection and self-referential memory allows us to reprogram the brain interaction with the rest of the body so that it is more helpful for our body balance. From my experience, hypnotherapy is an effective tool for such reprogramming. Clients consistently report that memories are more detailed and complete in hypnosis than when they think about them consciously.

Self-referential changes occur in memory, as well. When a client focuses on a memory associated with great fear *and reconstructs that event to no longer include the fear*, the client will almost always report a shift in visual perspective. As mentioned previously, the client first experiences the event from the first-person perspective, but after the fear is deleted, his vantage point changes to third person; thereafter, he just watches the event as if it were happening to anyone. With the greater emotional distance resulting from reconstructing that memory, fears regarding that event evaporate.

I can't tell you how many of my clients have been able to reduce or completely stop taking medications because after hypnotherapy sessions their symptoms just went away. And the changes are not transient; they do not wear off like the effects of medication, which must be taken repetitively to keep symptoms at bay. This is the difference between getting rid of the problem and enabling someone to handle a problem that remains. Not all clients can eliminate or at least reduce meds after doing hypnotherapy or other unconsciously driven interventions, of course, but a staggeringly large number of them can, which is consistent with the high percentage of psychosomatic issues that doctors see in their clinics.

As I mentioned previously, a physical problem requires a physical solution. A broken arm won't put itself back into the correct alignment by thinking about it or imagining it happening; it requires a mechanical manipulation to reposition the bone. Once that is done, however, healing can be supported and even accelerated using hypnotherapy. In a 1999 study, radiological exams of patients who received hypnotherapy as part of their healing program showed as much bone healing at week six as would typically take eight and a half weeks.[15] Pain, nausea, and other feelings of physical discomfort are reduced; likewise, feelings of anxiety, suffering, frustration, and other psychological discomfort. This is true for many physical and psychological symptoms associated with diagnoses including irritable bowel syndrome and all autoimmune illnesses, GERD, incontinence, asthma, allergies, COPD, and many more. Anything negatively impacted by increased arousal (too much stress) can be positively impacted using hypnotherapy, as it is ultimately a great way to reduce stress and keep it at a lower baseline level. The closer to healthy homeostasis arousal is, the more stressors it takes to increase it high enough to trigger symptoms of physical or psychological issues.

I must admit that I had my doubts about this idea early on in my hypnotherapy training. My trainers were all medical professionals, from Emergency Medical Technicians to physicians and clinical psychologists. I volunteered as a guinea pig for the medical-support section of the program, during which I had two weeks of hypnotherapy focusing on allergies that had caused me a lifetime of suffering. Because my arms swelled up so much, I was forced to take my allergy test in two sessions. I was allergic to basically everything. I'd taken allergy pills my whole life, eventually receiving several shots a couple of times each week for years. I even had surgery to remove nasal polyps and widen a sinus hole.

Honestly, I did not believe that hypnotherapy would make a dent in my issue. It seemed nothing could. I always assumed allergies were a purely biochemical problem, needing a chemical solution. Happily, after two weeks of hypnotherapy, during which I reconstructed past events including my parents' divorce and being adopted as a baby, I never had an allergy attack again. I'm very happy to have been proven wrong.

The brain researcher in me had to figure this out, and it actually made sense when I thought about it. A little bag of chemicals (baby) comes out of a big bag of chemicals (birth mom), to whom it is bonded chemically to allow it to survive. The big bag of chemicals goes away, and an alarm bell rings somewhere in the brain of the little bag of chemicals, as it cannot survive on its own. As it is no longer able to detect Mom's pheromones, an automatic survival response ensues. A few days later the little bag of chemicals goes home with a different big bag of chemicals (adopted mom) and lives happily ever after, but that doesn't change the fact that the alarm bell rang and its survival-related stress response was still programmed in that brain almost fifty years later, when it was, in essence, *un*-rung in hypnotherapy sessions by reconstructing the self-referential information and resulting processes that it initially constructed at the time of that event. Experiences as early as birth can strongly influence later maladaptive behavior.

From my experience of working with clients for over a decade, I have no doubt that being in a hypnotic state or otherwise focusing on unconscious processes affords immediate physical changes in brain structure that require no reinforcement to maintain. Bypassing rational brain activity enables us to make these kinds of changes. Often, lacking information, our rational, conscious minds are inadequate to help us understand how we feel and to make changes in present-time emotional or habitual brain processes. We have some great research from the neuroscience literature over the years concerning differences between the rational, language-oriented parts of the brain and the more visual, emotional parts. I believe that these cerebral asymmetries may correspond to differences in conscious-versus-unconscious–oriented brain-reprogramming strategies.

Chapter Four

Hemispheric Asymmetries and Consciousness

A WOMAN CAME TO me with a seemingly intractable fear of driving. She had been doing cognitive-behavioral therapy, including EMDR (eye movement desensitization and reprocessing), for three years. Her fear had not diminished. This quite-common fear while driving is usually easy to get rid of, typically a one-session fix in my office. We met three times, and she felt so much better. A year went by, and one day I saw her name on my schedule again. When she came in, she told me how much easier driving was for her until two weeks prior, when she suddenly caught herself feeling the urge to swerve into oncoming trucks.

She was not suicidal, she said, and the compulsive feeling to steer into oncoming traffic really scared her. She just couldn't come up with a rational explanation. She didn't want to die, for sure.

The fourth session, in which we focused on that terrifying impulse to swerve into traffic, resulted in a traumatic memory coming up for the first time since it happened when she was sixteen. Along with the memory a catharsis of emotion erupted, spilling out of her unconscious monster closet. Immediately after that traumatic experience originally occurred, she got in her car and drove five hours to a relative's house, feeling the whole way like swerving into oncoming traffic. Her fear of driving actually had nothing to do with driving per se; it was just an association. Because we focused on the *feeling she had while driving* instead of the driving itself, her brain could unlock that memory. That part of her brain came up with two words that stuck with her, "I matter." Whenever she thought about swerving her car into oncoming traffic after that, she immediately heard her mind say, "I matter," and the fleeting thought simply dissipated.

The next session focused on an event from her childhood in which her mother made her feel that she didn't matter. At the end of that session the memory was much dimmer, and the sadness it had produced had disintegrated. Another memory just popped into her head. It was her tenth birthday. She thought everyone had forgotten it, but some friends and family threw her a party, which made her feel that she *mattered*, she was *loved*. When she left my office, she felt excited, as she kept reflecting on that happy memory. Until that day she had not been able to bring up positive memories from her childhood easily, if at all. That was no longer a problem for her—nor was driving.

Just as a physical cause requires a physical solution, an unconscious psychological cause requires an unconscious psychological solution. It may seem obvious what the cause of a fear is, but if it's the conscious, rational mind that provides the answer, it may be wrong. In fact, in my experience it often is. And even when the conscious mind is correct, it can almost never eradicate that fear. You can understand a situation well and not change how you feel about it at all. A client who was well aware that her forty-year fear of public speaking stemmed from a single traumatic experience of giving a book report in school, during which the students laughed at her and her teacher said she was stupid, was still, no matter what she did, unable to erase that fear. But after one session using an unconscious-oriented protocol, she never had trouble with public speaking again. No longer afraid of being in front of an audience.

It is clear from neuroscience research—as well as what you've read in this book so far—that rational thought is much less powerful than we may want to think it is. Popular sayings like "Where there's a will there's a way" ingrain in us that once we set our minds to something, we can achieve it. We feel convinced that we have the capability to listen to our inner voice logically analyze a problem, produce a viable solution, and then execute that at will. This belief makes us feel comfortable, in control of all aspects of our lives: how we think, feel, and behave. This belief is wrong, so why do we hold it? It's as if we have two different minds in the same head, a rational one that we easily listen to and manipulate at will and another, under the surface, which does its own thing that we cannot control but that, in contrast, seems to control us. Most of us tend to personally identify with the voice of the rational mind, and any brain activity that doesn't agree with that is some other part of the brain that impacts us but is not us.

An amazing thing happens when a client is taught to move her attention from her inner voice (conscious mind) to her visual imagery and feelings (unconscious mind). I hear from a particular client every couple of years. It's the same each time, a long email explaining that she's blocked from doing something she wants to do and is self-sabotaging in some way, and all of the information about that block that she was able to find out from various sources. The latest block was that as an independent business owner, she atypically just couldn't bring herself to do much of the work necessary to make money and keep her business alive. Her email explained that she had been meditating on the issue every morning by asking herself a question about it, seeking out an answer. Also, she'd consulted her son, a clinical psychologist, who offered his best guess at what the problem could be, as well as her business coach and other family and friends.

My reply email read, "Stop. Just stop."

"That's like telling me not to breathe," was her response.

"I know. Take it as a personal challenge and make an appointment for a session so we can find out what's really going on." She did.

At the end of that session, she just laughed for a minute as she contemplated the solution that came up, which was completely different from what she and the other people she consulted thought it was. "I don't know why I'm surprised," she said. "This happens every time."

A couple more sessions, and she was no longer blocked.

All of her rational strategies for locating the cause of her block had failed, once again. Even when she meditated, her rational mind interceded, as trying to answer the question she meditated on engages the conscious mind. I see this all the time. Why? Does the brain not want us to find the right answers easily? Answering yes doesn't make much sense in terms of survival. As I keep emphasizing throughout this book, our brains appear to be protecting us all the time. Yet not getting the answers we need to facilitate better interactions with the world seems counterproductive.

Perhaps we're just asking the wrong part of the brain for answers it doesn't have. So it makes up apparently sensible answers that let us feel more in control so as to move forward in a more confident way. The problem with that approach, though, is that when the incorrect solution doesn't work, we feel even more powerless.

The rational mind (which sees us from a third-person perspective) and the self-referential mind (deeper, first-person perspective processing) are two separate systems or networks. We're a hybrid engine psychologically because our body (including our brain) is a hybrid engine. At any given time our body, including our brain, is dominated by either a high stress/sugar-burning/language-dominated (sympathetic nervous system) mode or a more relaxed/fat-burning/problem-solving mode (parasympathetic nervous system). When we use rational, logical, conscious strategies to find answers, we can gain understanding of what we're doing and how we want to change it, but that might not change how we feel about it one bit.

I see this all the time. A client will mention a traumatic event from the past and say, "I've dealt with it in therapy." When I ask how that client feels about it, tears well up. It may be hard to talk about. They haven't dealt with it completely, if at all. For instance, one client can't even think about happy memories of her mother, who passed away ten years ago, because she's so upset over losing her. Still. Clearly, she's still actively mourning the loss. If a change we want to make comes from an emotional cause, we have to interact directly with the unconscious part of the brain, run by the Default Mode Network, that controls our interoception, our arousal and affect. Once we focus on the emotional part and hear what it has to tell us, then reprogram it to clear the maladaptive feelings, we can rid ourselves of negative feelings and overarousal, leading to benefits such as being able to find joy in thinking about and talking about memories of someone we've lost.

A client I'll call David was plagued with especially violent memories from his military service that he'd completely repressed, shoved into a mental closet because they were too emotionally difficult to remember.

He told me that whenever he thought about a particular time, he felt sick to his stomach. He was unable to pull up any memories from then, so he didn't understand why he felt so upset. Using techniques directed toward his unconscious mind, we went directly to the part of the brain that was causing the stomachache and listened to what it was trying to tell him—that he had unresolved feelings of anger at having watched the parents of a young girl murdered in front of her. Going back to this experience, he reconstructed it in his brain nonemotionally, changing the affect from negative to neutral and reducing the arousal level it caused. At the end of the session, he said that he was able to think consciously about that troubling event, remembering it fully and neutrally, for the first time ever without any stomach pain.

The conscious mind, not having insight into the part of the brain that has the correct answers about unconscious issues, comes up with a rational explanation, trying to help, but is often wrong. Michael Gazzaniga, who worked with Roger Sperry to help us understand where control of various processes are located in the brain, came up with the idea of an *interpreter*. It makes a lot of sense in light of my work and is backed up by current research.[16] According to him, a part of the brain, situated in the left cerebral hemisphere, interprets unconscious brain activity, making it understandable to us consciously. When we listen to that interpreter part of the brain, which communicates with us via language (our inner voice), we are not listening to the area of the brain that knows what's up; rather, we're listening to an intermediary. It's like playing an old game of Telephone, using cans and string. With each successive person who passes the information, as it goes around a circle, the information gets more widely variant from the original message; in the end, it may even be way off. Its construction and reconstruction will be influenced to varying degrees by other factors that skew the interpretation, such as beliefs and needs, other people's reactions to it when we discuss it with them, and additional relevant facts.[17]

There is an interesting seeming contradiction that we see in hypnotherapy concerning language and consciousness. For achieving a hypnotic state on demand in a practitioner's office, quieting that inner voice is important. It helps for us to switch our attention from the interpreter to our self-referential (DMN) processes. We do this spontaneously throughout the day without the aid of what hypnotherapists call an *induction* (e.g., imagining we are going down a flight of steps) to help us switch focus and enter a hypnotic state. By quieting that inner voice, we stop listening to the conscious mind, turning our attention to visual images and feelings (the unconscious mind). Though this process of "turning off the conscious mind" uses language, the rational mind is no longer in charge. Even while the hypnotherapy practitioner reads the client a script or asks the client to describe how he feels emotionally and/or physically when he imagines a particular mental movie playing in front of him, he is switching to unconscious-mind dominance.

More often than not, the part of the client that has the answers we need doesn't use language at all. In such cases, we can enable unconscious communication via *ideomotor signaling*—that is, let the client's unconscious mind "speak" via a body signal. Hypnotherapists commonly use this communication hack with great success. For example, I wanted to talk with a part of a client's brain that was blocking him from achieving a goal and asked, in hypnosis, if that part would speak to me. The client shook his head no. I asked if it would be okay for that part to lift the client's right index finger to indicate yes and the left index finger for no. The client nodded. Then the nonverbal part began to communicate. In this way, we were able to understand the true cause of the block and reprogram it.

This duality in mental processing makes sense in light of hemispheric asymmetries and cerebral dominance. The big, wrinkly part of the brain, the *cerebrum*, is divided into two halves and sits on top of brain structures essential to more automatic physical processes, such as heart rate and respiration. The two cerebral halves, called *hemispheres*, look the same and perform many of the same or similar functions, but in neither structure nor function are they identical.

Some epilepsy patients benefit greatly from a surgery called a *callosectomy*, in which the largest bundle of nerve fibers connecting the two halves of the brain is severed, greatly reducing the communication between the two hemispheres. Via back roads, there is still some interaction, but the freeway is out. The fascinating studies that Sperry and Gazzaniga did with these so-called "split-brain" patients provided a lot of information about the different functions of the two hemispheres (or two brains) and how they work together. This work was so influential that Sperry was awarded the Nobel Prize for it in 1981.

In these split-brain cases, the two hemispheres behave very much like two separate minds. For example, when a patient looks through her clothes closet to get dressed, the right hand may pick out one shirt while the left hand, which is controlled by the opposite hemisphere, grabs a different shirt.

In a more dramatic condition, called *alien hand syndrome*, the *left hand, controlled by the more emotionally dominant right brain*, may even go as far as trying to strangle the patient's pet or trying to choke the patient herself to get its point across!

In cases like this, the right hemisphere, apparently frustrated by being ignored, acts out like a petulant child. That hemisphere communicates primarily with images, feelings, and actions—not language. The left hemisphere, on the other hand, relies heavily on language. In Sperry's controlled lab studies with these split-brain patients, we can see just how much we humans depend on language and how difficult it can be for us to "hear" the right hemisphere. In a classic experiment that nicely illustrates this idea, a split-brain patient sits in front of a screen that shows a picture of a snow scene to the left of center and a chicken foot to the right. The information in the left visual field goes to the right hemisphere and vice versa, so the right hemisphere sees only the snow scene and the left hemisphere only the chicken foot. Asked what he sees, the patient answers "a chicken foot" because the left hemisphere talks; the right hemisphere does not.

The patient also has eight pictures of various objects in front of him. When asked to point to the picture that goes with what he saw on the screen, his right hand points to a chicken. Because his left hand, however, is controlled by the right hemisphere, which saw the snow scene, it points to a shovel. When the patient is asked why he pointed to a snow shovel, he responds, "to clean out the chicken coop." *The right hemisphere could not tell the left about the snow scene because the communication freeway was closed, so the left hemisphere (rational, conscious mind) had to come up with a story to explain the shovel, which was there to remove the snow.*

But even in intact brains, we hypnotherapists see this *interhemispheric-communication issue* all the time. Our conscious mind, or "interpreter" per Gazzaniga, in the left hemisphere, we listen to as our "inner voice." That "voice," in my view, is a survival mechanism, not the real "us."

It makes up stories *to make the world make sense*, to make us feel better (reduce our confusion-induced arousal and improve our body budget), so that we can more easily survive to the next day. But even when that neural highway is running smoothly—intact—our conscious mind is not privy to a lot of the information it needs from the right hemisphere, in which the real "you" resides. Therefore, it often has no insight into how you *really* feel or what you *really* want. It cannot peel away the layers that deep, as the right-brain information does. That part of you is completely unconscious and cannot talk.

We can see this miscommunication in action when a client verbalizes a thought with a simultaneous little slow shake of her head, for example. Or when she says she wants to do something, but her legs and arms cross while she's saying it. When I draw my clients' attention to a behavior like that, they often produce an embarrassed laugh, as they had not been aware of the behavior.

The two halves of the brain can do many of the same things. But when both are activated, one hemisphere is going to be in charge. This is called cerebral dominance. Having both in charge at the same time is not biologically productive, so when both are sharing a task, one hemisphere is in control. For a more language-based task, the left hemisphere is likely dominant. For a more visual or emotional task, the right hemisphere would be a better choice to lead the charge and make the decisions.

Hypnotherapy and other unconscious-oriented protocols are focused on helping the client change maladaptive emotional programming and behavior. We want to help her get what she *really* wants, not just what she *says* she wants, which may be two different things. She may say she wants to quit smoking, but perhaps she's trying to convince herself of that just because her husband and kids really want her to quit. Their wishes may be at odds with her wishes. She may really enjoy it. Her conscious mind tries to get her to stop, using patches and medications and willpower—all for naught. She may be frustrated, not clear why her attempts keep failing or why she gives up the habit temporarily, only to pick up a cigarette again almost reflexively when a stressful event occurs. All smokers I've met have quit repeatedly. The trick to staying quit is to reprogram the need behind that behavior. The cause of that smoking behavior was part of an automatic stress-reduction intent dominated by the right hemisphere, for which left-hemisphere devised treatment was ineffective.

So if our core self-referential wants and needs are dominated by the right hemisphere, why do we pay so much more attention to the left? That conscious mind seems to be the default for our attentional spotlight, to such an extent that the left hemisphere has long been referred to as the *dominant* hemisphere and the right the *nondominant* hemisphere. I think there's good reason for this. The answer lies in how essential words are to us humans. For our concept development, we need them. We are not born with the concept of "dog" or "anger"; we construct and reconstruct them as we interact with others and in particular situations in which we hear those words. In fact, in individuals who have a condition called *alexithymia*, in which they are unable to recognize, identify, and describe their emotions, social development is hindered. Even individuals without this condition can sometimes have difficulty in this regard, which may negatively impact conscious-driven therapies but not affect unconscious-driven interventions, as the latter does not rely on language. The important thing for clients to be able to do in unconscious-oriented protocols is to feel discomfort. These interventions are focused not on reconstructing emotional concepts but rather *changing feelings that, through emotionally charged events, have been associated with concepts*. Hypnosis may therefore be a right-hemisphere–dominated process.

Asking hypnotized people to describe their emotions and body sensations is a helpful way to draw their attentional focus to how they feel. Left hemisphere language and other processes are essential to hypnotherapy even though right-hemisphere processes dominate and direct the overall whole-brain activity. So it does not necessarily follow that using language in this way engages left-hemisphere language processes and conscious activity only, to the point of switching processes in our hybrid psychological engine. Similarly, describing an event briefly or engaging in an imaginary dialog with someone who hurt you tends to keep the client in a hypnotic state; the two hemispheres are connected and functioning together, with the right dominant while in that altered hypnotic state of consciousness. In fact, one of the benefits of right-hemisphere domination is *increased interaction* between the two hemispheres. In contrast, when the left brain is in charge, there is less interaction between the two—actual inhibition of right-hemisphere processing and more concentration on left-brain–dominant processes.

This decreased interactivity can perhaps be explained by the fact that the left brain engages in more step-by-step processing—serially—whereas with right-brain–dominant tasks, we see more parallel processing: many processes running unconsciously simultaneously. But, as I've mentioned before, this spares us. If we were aware of that parallel activity, we would be completely overwhelmed, unable to interact with our world.

This makes right-hemisphere dominance essential for problem-solving and creative thought, as it associates many concepts all at once without the strict, conscious information filtering and selectivity. Relying on left-hemisphere serial processes would not allow for such a variety of associations. *We would start with what worked for us previously and come up with a variation on that rather than something innovative.*

As Einstein famously said, *"If at first the idea is not absurd, there is no hope for it."* When you shift from left-brain–dominant activity and let the right take over, as in hypnosis, you expand your narrow attentional spotlight to more of a lantern, a metaphor originally proposed by John Flavell and used by developmental psychologist Alison Gopnik to describe children's awareness of the outer world. An attentional lantern allows you to distribute your attention more globally and evenly, as contrasted with a spotlight, which allows you to pay attention selectively to what you think is important and ignore everything else.[18]

In high stress you narrow your focus, which can make it more difficult for people to go into a hypnotic state on demand. Reducing stress using unconscious-focused techniques gives us more real control by putting the right hemisphere in charge of more processes again without interference from that somewhat clueless left brain. Mental clarity increases as our reliance on left-hemisphere–dominant processes decreases. Additional memories, images, and feelings come up more easily when our attention is more diffusely open to manifestations of unconscious communication.

I recently saw a fascinating possible example of this in a long-time client. She was raised in a family of mentally ill individuals and recently realized that she grew up with sexual and emotional abuse, which she was taught was normal and acceptable. Sixty-some years later, about a year after ridding herself of dissociation that kept her in the dark about her abuse, she told me at the end of a session that she was able to feel a pain in her left side as she worked her way through some reprogramming. What amazed me was her next statement – "That was the first time I've ever been able to feel any pain on the left side of my body." It was not a neurological problem; she could feel normal sensation on her left side when she paid attention to it, but when she wasn't thinking about it she only felt discomfort on her right side. Her right brain controls the left side of her body and dominates emotional activity. Had it been keeping her attention away from a lifetime of discomfort, both physical and emotional, by somehow numbing the pain and suffering whenever possible, extending to all physical discomfort on her left side? Earlier I mentioned that hypnosis may work for pain mediation by keeping those uncomfortable feelings out of our awareness. Her situation seemed to be an attentional one, as well.

And this was not the first time she experienced this kind of attentional numbness. She recalled a time in her life when she could not feel any discomfort in her body if it was below her waist. She had been actively working on some emotional issues using more consciously directed therapy but was not aware of her past sexual abuse at the time, so the connection was not made.

Now that she has done some major memory and concept reconstruction to make her reality more consistent with her current life, she is finally aware of the abuse in her past and her brain is starting to allow her to feel pain everywhere, whether she is paying attention to it or not. It's as though she has banished enough monsters from the closet that the ones left are seen as manageable, unpleasant but no longer overwhelming. Some of the defensive walls, such as dissociation and attentional numbness, can finally come down, and the chatter in her head continues to diminish.

When resistance or blockage to unconscious processes is lifted, which many hypnotherapists refer to as a softening of the *critical factor* (that boundary between the conscious and subconscious minds), hypnosis is likely to be possible. This represents, to me and others, the shift from left- to right-hemisphere dominance. Some people—creatives and children, for example—spend a lot of time in a right-hemisphere–dominant state. That this is the case with children may indicate that this hemisphere is, in essence, dominant for most processes and that left-hemisphere dominance develops more in those people most focused on their rational mental processes ("living in their head," listening to that inner voice). Yet most processes throughout our entire brain are not rational and therefore may be more right-hemisphere driven—begging the question: for most mental and physical processes, is the right side of our brain the *truly* dominant hemisphere?

Chapter Five

Outsmarting the Brain

ONE OF MY CLIENTS had great success losing weight as a result of our sessions. I saw her a few months after we finished work, and she told me that in the last couple of weeks she'd ruined all the progress we'd made. At least, it felt that way. I asked her what happened, and she said she had an upcoming surgery; she didn't think she was that worried about it but must be; oh, and she had a fight with her husband, but the surgery was constantly on her mind. She even had nonstop stomach pains from the tension.

After she talked for a while about her surgery worries, I asked about the fight with her husband. It stood out instantly to me as "off," a non sequitur. She rushed through recounting it, minimizing its importance with words, tone, and a nonverbal shake of the head. She said she'd seen an ugliness in her husband she hadn't seen before. Immediately following the fight she took a nap, and upon waking she had a feeling that her future was in jeopardy. I asked her if she would be okay with investigating that feeling. She said she didn't know why I would want to, but she was game.

During her induction to help her into a hypnotic state, I led her down some steps and had her get in touch with that feeling she had when she woke up from her nap. I had her label the emotions and physical sensations she felt. When I asked her to give the feeling a form or shape, she mentioned a small fist in her stomach. I had her take it out of her body, and then a memory came to her. She was just a few years old and in a car with a couple of older boys who were talking about sexually assaulting her. Another boy made sure they got her home safely, but she said that was when she learned there was ugliness in the world (you see the association with the ugliness she saw in her husband when they fought). The image she saw to represent the feeling in the car was a big man's fist in her stomach, and she made that go away. Her stomach pain went with it.

When she was fully back in the room with me, she told me that she'd seen a little girl, whom she assumed was her, in a blue dress running through a meadow, catching butterflies (opposite to the feeling of being trapped in the car, her future in jeopardy), and that the same little girl had led her down the steps during her induction. Her unconscious mind knew what the real issue was that needed to be reprogrammed, and it wasn't her husband or her upcoming surgery. The fight brought back that old feeling that was a major stressor sixty years prior, a program still running, even though she hadn't thought about that incident since it happened. When she left my office, she felt really good, emotionally and physically. She had no worries and was looking forward to seeing her husband.

Strategies like the ones illustrated above that tap directly into unconscious processes can enable clients to quickly and easily reconstruct their life stories, reducing the arousal value of their memories of those events and changing the affect from negative to neutral or even positive. Those interoceptive changes are beneficial to their body budgets and alter future predictions that their brains make about situations that used to be associated with negative, stressful programming. In the above example, listening, the way we do as coaches, allowed me to pick up on the bit of negative information she expressed about the fight with her husband that didn't fit with her story about the anxiety over her upcoming surgery. That was a window into an unconscious concern her brain was bringing to her attention, even though her conscious mind had deemed it unimportant. It was important enough that those filtering and selection mechanisms were not able to keep it from being expressed. But it didn't fit with the conscious mind's fabricated story about what her issue was.

Bringing her attention to what her unconscious mind was trying to tell her and letting it lead her to the real problem, using a combination of coaching, hypnosis, and NLP, allowed her to more positively reconstruct her memory of that traumatic childhood event. Any future events that could be even obliquely associated with that old memory will no longer elicit negative feelings or overreactions from that reconstructed memory because the negative, stressful feelings are no longer embedded in that associated memory. She has emotional distance from them now, which positively impacts her body budget.

Looking for non sequiturs is just one way of listening to what the unconscious mind may be trying to tell us. A *parapraxis*, or "Freudian slip," is easy for a listener to pick up on but not always detected by the speaker. In conversation, one of my clients referred to her father as a rapist, but when I asked her why she used that label, she didn't recall saying it. Investigating it further, I found out that she had been raped by her father when she was young. I had worked with her for three years, and this was her first reference to this series of events. It had been pushed down so deeply into her monster closet that it took that long for her brain to be ready to process it.

There are also nonverbal ways that important unconscious information can make it to the surface. When a client talks about wanting to stop drinking as she crosses her arms and legs, then laughs in surprise when I bring to her attention that she just twisted herself up like a pretzel, her unconscious mind is telling her that part of her doesn't really want to stop drinking. Her brain may be using that behavior as a coping mechanism for a bigger issue, in which case it may freak out if that coping mechanism is removed.

We don't get what we *want*; we get what we *focus on and expect*. Once we focus on listening to our unconscious mind, we can get more accurate information about how we *really* feel and what we *really* need. Once we understand what the real issue is, we can reframe our expectations. A longtime client told me recently that she really resented her roommates for making her pick up after them. She felt disrespected because she thought everyone should clean up after themselves; that way, she would have less work. I introduced a perspective shift simply by asking her if she thought that cleaning up after themselves was important to her roommates. She said obviously not; they didn't care that the place was a mess. She was cleaning up because she wanted a clean house, not because they cared whether it was clean or not. She was doing it for herself, not them. I could see the light bulb go on over her head as she smiled; the long-held resentment had instantly vanished.

Even at times when they don't get rid of the underlying issues themselves, perspective shifts can be handy for eradicating blocks. I had a smoking-cessation client who was so dependent on nicotine that whenever he couldn't smoke, he had to have a nicotine patch on him or be chewing nicotine gum to have a constant flow of nicotine into his body. He had tried everything; nothing worked. Some questioning revealed that one of his greatest pleasures was a weekly get-together with his friends at a cigar bar. Valuing the secondary gain of bonding with his buddies through smoking cigars, his unconscious mind had been sabotaging his efforts to give up nicotine.

I asked him if he would like to give up the cigarettes, patches, and gum—just smoke cigars once a week with his friends. He was shocked to hear me ask that and told me he thought he had to give up smoking completely, all or nothing, but that yes, he would love to be able to limit his nicotine intake to just that activity. The new idea shifted his expectation to a plan that excited him and that his unconscious mind supported. We did a few sessions, and then he woke up the morning of his self-imposed quit date, lying in bed, staring at the ceiling, waiting for the nicotine craving to kick in. After a while he got up and poured himself a cup of coffee, which always made him want to smoke, but still felt no craving. He went to work and had none the entire day. The craving had gone completely.

That weekend, golfing with his buddies, he told them about his experience. They said he was full of it and lying to them. They couldn't believe what he reported was possible. But for almost a year he didn't smoke or use any nicotine except cigars with his buddies. Some of his friends started trickling in to see me themselves to stop smoking. Others tried to tempt him to smoke again. He eventually gave in, and this time, returning to my office, he didn't want to smoke cigars, either. He wanted to be the epitome of health. In only a couple of sessions he reprogrammed the core of the issue, reconstructed his self-concept, and became a nonsmoker for life.

This approach worked when all others failed because he shifted his perspective to take his unconscious needs and wants into account. He saw a new possibility that his entire brain could support. All of his brain was on the same page, moving toward that goal, with no part putting up resistance. We found a middle ground, which for a long while he made work. Eventually, though, he had to change that goal. He was able to quit smoking completely, having proven to himself that he didn't need to smoke to be an effective worker and feel good about himself, and that increase in self-confidence and self-empowerment and the reconstruction of his self-concept fueled a complete life transformation that went way beyond getting off of the nicotine.

A perspective shift can remodel our expectations and predictions about ourselves in the world. And when our brains detect less prediction error as a consequence of those modified interactions, we increase our feelings of being understood and accepted, which positively impacts our body budget. In the above example, a perspective shift kicked off a series of unconscious-oriented interventions that resulted in the permanent changes the client wanted, but something intermediate had to happen. The perspective shift alone was not enough. It just opened the door to making the changes.

Moving and broadening our attentional spotlight to focus on unconscious information by silencing that conscious voice allows us to shift habitual behaviors more easily than trying to force-feed them to ourselves. It's like taking the lid off a pot so that what we want to put in there actually gets in. This even works with language-oriented strategies, such as suggestions. As long as the suggestion or affirmation is short, positive, and in the present tense, we can use it for what I call brute-force reprogramming. Giving yourself a suggestion repetitively can be very effective, but it will usually be more impactful if you start by silencing that inner voice (taking the lid off the pot). Being in a hypnotic state is not necessary to reap the benefits of suggestions, or mantras, or affirmations, but an overwhelming majority of my clients have noted that it feels different; apparently, the change they wanted to make got to a deeper, more transformative level.

A great way to see this in action is to give a few suggestions to a child while he's sleeping and his unconscious mind is in charge. Whenever I have clients with small children who are struggling with something, such as bed-wetting, I help them craft suggestions that let the kids feel more in control, loved, and anything else that counteracts what the parents have noticed is negatively impacting them. Following the very first night of giving the positive suggestions to their children, these parents report a reduction in the troubling thoughts, feelings and/or behaviors or a complete elimination of them.

Changing our self-talk, the internal dialogs we have with ourselves, is another way to immediately alter how we feel. This conscious strategy promotes unconscious change in stress level and emotion. To rewrite one of your life stories or reconstruct a mental concept, it may not be enough, but it may help open a door to doing so, using other tools. When we stop the processing of a negative thought in its tracks and then reframe it positively, we can start to shift our perspective on that issue. We also realize that whatever trash we are talking to ourselves is, in fact, indicating a block that isn't being addressed. Your brain is not pointing out how your life sucks in order to make you feel hopeless, as that would not help your body budget. Rather, your brain uses negative thoughts and feelings to draw your attention to *what you can change* in your life to improve it and positively affect your body budget. It's pointing out opportunities.

An easy way to start changing how you talk to yourself is, when you have a negative thought, to say "Cancel, cancel" to yourself and restate the thought in a positive way. For example, if you hear yourself say, "I can't do this yoga pose," say "Cancel, cancel. I am doing this yoga pose better every day." After a short time, you will get used to that positiveness, and your brain will start making those scripts automatically (unconsciously)!

There is an imagery-based version of this exercise that helps with negative feelings as well. When you have a negative feeling about an event that you're visualizing—say, a task you're dreading—you can use what we call a *break state* (under closed eyelids, move your eyeballs up, down, side-to-side, and straight ahead) and then use an *anchor* to give yourself a good feeling. An anchor is a handy-dandy little NLP tool by which you program an association (add a new neural connection) between a good feeling and, say, touching your thumb and index finger together, so that when you touch those fingers together, you call the good feeling back.

You can then, by intention, associate this good feeling with future events you imagine. That way, you're likely to go into those events feeling better than otherwise. You can change your expectations by changing your affect from negative to positive or neutral, making that task feel more doable, which increases the probability that you'll do it, removing that mental block.

You can feel a perspective shift and the stress that results from it with another simple little exercise. Close your eyes and tell yourself you have to do something—say, the dishes—that you don't like, "I should do the dishes," or, "I need to do the dishes." Feel your stress increasing. Now change it to, "I *want* to do the dishes." Feels different, right? That's because your brain processes those words differently. Instead of adding something to the pile of stuff you have to do, building stress and throwing off your body budget, you're giving yourself an opportunity that positively impacts your body budget. And it's not lying to yourself, because even if you don't like doing the dishes, you like having clean dishes to use. So ultimately what you're telling yourself is true. You want to do the dishes.

Lying to yourself, on the other hand, doesn't work at all. If you hate working out but try to tell yourself you like going to the gym, you'll fail. Why? Because you're talking to yourself, and you know you're lying! There's a sneaky way around this, though. Outsmart your brain by adding—in front of the statement—"more and more now." Just those four words. "More and more now, I like going to the gym." Your brain will quite possibly accept that suggestion because you're saying that you're in the process of liking it, which might be true. It's not sure, and in the confusion the suggestion sneaks in under the radar, changing your expectations, altering your brain's predictions, and making it easier for you to get yourself to the gym.

Our expectations are predictions that our unconscious minds construct and then reconstruct in light of prediction errors. Our brains don't care if we're really doing something or just imagining it: the same reprogramming occurs. *Imagery involves the same brain processes as actually interacting with the world,* save the motor execution and external sensory feedback. This makes visual imagery so effective for changing thoughts, feelings, and behaviors. Fake-it-till-you-make-it works great for brain reprogramming.

Visual information has survival value for us humans, as we are tall animals and therefore rely on vision more than any other sense. My own research has shown that we attend to information presented to our upper visual field, or the visual information that comes into the top half of our eyes, more quickly than information in our lower visual field.[19] If there is something bigger than we are within our visual range, we better see it and learn all we can about it as quickly as possible, as it may be a threat. I also found an indication that we *attend* to information in our left visual field (which goes to the right brain, or hemisphere) faster than information in our right visual field (which goes to the left brain), perhaps because the right side of the brain is dominant for getting and processing information quickly, by running many processes simultaneously, to determine if we need to be concerned about it or not. Conversely, information in the right visual field that goes to the left side of the brain is *remembered* better, perhaps because that hemisphere is dominant for naming and categorizing that information.

Engaging right-hemisphere control in the process of shifting our attention to potentially important information allows us to listen to what our unconscious minds want us to change. There are many ways to prime the right brain to take charge. Silencing that inner voice is very effective. It doesn't keep us from being able to use language; it just shifts the leadership of brain activity from left to right temporarily. Doodling with the left hand, for example, or focusing on visual images helps to keep brain-activity dominance on the right side and forms the basis of the unconscious strategies we use to help people make changes that they have been unable to make.

One of the most effective protocols I use starts with the client daydreaming about a comfortable place—real or imagined—seeing a mental movie in which they interact with that comfortable world. They move without pain, engaging in movements that they have not been able to perform due to discomfort. In this environment, they are able to dial down the amount of pain that they feel—with an imaginary dial to which their bodies immediately respond—and prove to themselves that they don't actually have to feel that discomfort. This technique changes the client's body budget predictions, influencing the brain's simulation of pain, and even changes feedback from the rest of the body regarding that pain via top-down neural connections that modulate the processing of bottom-up pain information.

I'll never forget my first house call, when I witnessed the healing power of imagination. In desperation, a woman who was in so much pain from a recent back surgery that she couldn't even get out of bed to go to the bathroom called me. Less than an hour later, as our session ended, she had dialed her pain down to zero. She walked with no issues, in complete comfort, to the kitchen to get me a check.

We can use imagery to make all sorts of brain changes. This is because the brain takes imagery seriously; to the brain it's just as real as the action it imagines.[20] This opens up a whole world of possible healing tools, including but not limited to hypnotherapy. Earlier I mentioned neurolinguistic programming (NLP). Some of the most effective image-based strategies I have used are NLP tools. They can quickly and easily help people make drastic changes. Though the name implies that these tools are language-based, they rely heavily on imagery.

My all-time favorite NLP protocol uses imagery to create emotional distance from a traumatic event so that it's easier to reprogram. I detailed a case using this technique earlier in this book—the woman who was so afraid of dinosaurs that at the sight of a life-sized replica of a brontosaurus on the side of the road she almost crashed a car full of people. When she initially told me about this event, she was hyperventilating. I had her imagine a short movie clip of the traumatic event, then let it go. I explained that we'd come back to it later but in an easier way. When we brought that movie clip back up later, it was in black and white with no sound or feelings—thus, creating emotional distance—and she was not even watching it; she floated out of her body, which remained in the theater seat, and watched the back of her head as the imaginary her watched the movie clip—creating even more emotional distance. We added a calm or happy lead-in and conclusion, so she started and ended the movie on a good note. Then we had her step into the end of the film and enjoy that happy clip before running the movie backwards really fast. Add to that an amusing sound as the movie ran backwards, and after a few repetitions all that remained with her were the good feelings at the beginning and end of the movie, which seemed to collapse on top of and delete the negative feelings from the traumatic event in between. She tried to bring up that panicky feeling again but couldn't.

Imagery also lets us create a mentally stressful condition known as *cognitive dissonance*, which can facilitate a change in belief. Cognitive dissonance occurs when someone's beliefs and actions don't line up. When a client is describing a traumatic event and their body shows increased arousal and negative affect, we can encourage them to shift their attention, focusing on locating that feeling in their body, then describing it fully, drawing attention away from reviewing the trauma itself. Looking around in my office, they can see that they are safe, *which is at odds with the belief from the imagery that they are not safe.* The two beliefs cannot exist together while imagining that event. They see that they cannot change the fact that they are safe, so the body response of fear does not make sense. Automatically, then, the belief that drives that fearful response is changed. Maybe they experience a cathartic release of emotion, such as crying, that quickly goes away, the body response goes away, and they can now think and talk about that past event without the survival-related fear that always accompanied it.

One of my clients started talking about the first time her ex-husband raped her. Emotion got the better of her, resulting in her talking faster, breathing heavily, and her voice changed noticeably to that of a scared girl. She seemed to be reverting to the event in her mind, or perhaps to an even earlier event when she was abused as a child by her father. I always want my clients to *review* past events, *not relive them*. So I asked her to open her eyes.

She looked surprised to be in my office. I told her, "Tell me if you're safe." Her eyes canvassed the room, and she said yes, she was safe. I asked if she was okay. "Yes," she said again, she was. At the end of our session she felt like a huge weight had been lifted, a weight she had carried around for many years. Now, when thinking about that event, she felt empowered, not unsafe, having made the positive body budget change that resulted from processing that event. A change that remains to this day.

The body's default is to move toward balance, and any tools that help it get there tend to be very fast and effective. There may be many ways that we can rewrite our life stories to release negative mental influences on our body budget. Unconscious-oriented brain hacks tap into natural brain strategies, and we should see them as viable options for anyone to try, especially people who have not been successful with other approaches.

Chapter Six

Hypnotherapy

HYPNOSIS ON DEMAND IS a very helpful brain hack to quickly and accurately get to the cause of an issue. Very often I witness clients surprised by the causes they discover at the root of their issues. They are usually quite different from what they expected. Research has not provided evidence that people in hypnosis can go back in time to an event that caused an issue, or that people can retrieve memories using hypnosis,[21] but every hypnotherapist I know has witnessed both of these things many, many times. In my office I experience them almost daily. The assertion that this is possible goes back to Freud and Breuer in the late 1800s. According to them, trauma results in repressed, or buried, emotions. Remember our discussion of blocks and closets. These emotions, which weren't expressed at what we call the "initial sensitizing event," or ISE, today continue to cause disturbances in thoughts, feelings, and/or behaviors, and hypnosis allows the client to uncover them in their entirety. This *catharsis* can resolve symptoms that weren't resolved with hypnotic suggestions alone.

It's fascinating to discuss an issue with a client and hear what their conscious mind has to say about it, then in hypnosis get an entirely different picture as new information comes up of which the client was not aware. How do we know which narrative, if either, is correct? That answer is simple: because *after reprogramming the emotional information brought up with the event in hypnosis*, the client feels different—now having more emotional distance from it, and that distance remains. The client does not revert to feeling as he did previously. The memory is structurally, neurally, reconstructed in the brain—no longer having the personally intense or negative feelings and maladaptive behaviors attached to it, a now-unimportant event that is in fact no longer personally relevant. The client can leave the past in the past.

The research that looked unfavorably or apprehensively at regression (or helping a client mentally go back to a previous event) does not take into account that modern hypnotherapists, unlike Freud and Breuer, do not necessarily try to get a client to *relive* a past event; rather, we want them to *review* the event. We want them to see it as if they are a fly on the wall, watching a younger version of themselves in whatever event their unconscious minds take them back to. Occasionally, clients can appear to actually be reliving an event, and in those cases we have them come back to the sound of our voice, and in a relaxed state refocus on simply reviewing the event.

One of my clients brought a friend in to see me because in a few days she had to give court testimony as the victim of a violent crime. While she slept, her boyfriend had shot her with a shotgun. The sound of the blast woke her up, and she noticed that her internal organs were exposed. Having fuzzy memories of that event, she thought there might have been a second man involved. To ascertain whether another violent offender was out there somewhere, it was imperative that she remember the event as accurately as possible.

We did an *analytical hypnotherapy* session, typically called *regression therapy*. I don't like the term *regression* or the term *therapy* because of the possible confusion with psychotherapy regression techniques, during which clients are encouraged to actually go into the past and *relive* traumatic events. I instructed her to review the event in question, and she started hyperventilating. I reminded her that she was perfectly safe and that I wanted her to just review the event like she was a fly on the wall. Her breathing instantly returned to a deep, slow, relaxed rate. Then I had her describe the event from the beginning, when she heard the gunshot, and she complied with a calm play-by-play of the entirety of it up until the doors closed on the ambulance that took her to the hospital. Then I helped her back to complete consciousness, at which point she remembered everything, as clear as day in a continuous account, with no hesitation, no pauses to think. She also understood why she wondered whether there might have been a second man there. Her boyfriend's demeanor drastically changed after he shot her; he became very sweet and helpful, calling 911 and trying to keep her calm until the police and fire departments arrived. That behavior was so at odds with the violence he expressed right beforehand that she thought there might have been two separate attackers.

The brain can hide a negative event so completely that there are no indications of it at all, sometimes not since the event occurred. More so than in the example above, the brain of one client was particularly adept at this. When I started to induce him into a hypnotic state, his brain would take over and immediately put him into a deep state of trance without my help. When he came back into the room at the end of a session, he would have no memory of the session at all, which is unusual. As I've said before, how deeply someone goes into a hypnotic state or whether they even go into that state is completely up to them. Their brain is in charge throughout.

During one session a memory came to him. He could smell rubber, as from a raft, and felt extremely angry. Then his brain went somewhere else, and I followed. After our session, I inquired about that anger and rubber smell. He had not even the slightest hint as to what I was talking about. At his next session I asked if he would like to investigate that anger; he agreed. When in hypnosis, he was able to give me a bright, rich, detailed description of his mental movie. He was in a rubber raft with several other guys, and from a riverbank someone was throwing human body parts at them. This so inflamed him that he tried to get out of the raft and over to the guy to make him stop, which naturally could have been life threatening. He could smell the rubber under his nose as the other guys in the raft pinned him down, preventing any further movement. I helped him release the anger and reconstruct that memory, after which his sleep improved, which is what he came to me for in the first place.

Usually, though, clients in hypnosis are familiar with the event they bring up; it's related to an issue they may be painfully aware of. In a minority of cases, they know the cause but cannot completely reconstruct it on their own. Hypnosis offers a helping hand to allow the client to listen to unconscious information that has not been making it up to their consciousness, providing them greater awareness and understanding of the issue and allowing them to easily reduce or eliminate its negative influence on their body budget.

Generally speaking, hypnosis is labeled a state of altered consciousness, as is meditation, though the concept of mental "state" is ambiguous. A hypnotic induction starts out as meditation. The client establishes a focus, such as by taking a few deep, slow breaths and/or feeling their body sink into the chair. To meditate, they focus their attention on something (e.g., their breathing), and when the mind naturally moves away from that to something more interesting, they gently move their attention back to the object of focus. Brain waves shift from fully-awake beta to relaxed alpha. When the client is nice and relaxed, in the meditative state, then we let the mind wander, bringing up whatever it wants to, showing us what it's important to address in the moment.

This shifting of mental activity to listening to what the unconscious mind is trying to tell us turns the process from meditation to hypnosis, and though the client remains visually relaxed,

we see their brain waves shift from alpha back to beta. Research shows this change in brain waves in all areas of the cerebrum and in both hemispheres, indicating greater overall cognitive activity, as is the case when the right brain is in control.[22] The hypnotized client exhibits the brain waves of being awake, unlike in meditation, but maintains the outward signs of being in that altered state. This is why I refer to hypnosis as *meditation on steroids*—our brains are *more* active, getting more work done with all of that parallel processing.

To determine if someone is in hypnosis, we can look for signs; for example, lacrimation (unemotional eye watering), time distortion, and a silenced inner voice. But we don't always see any signs. We can notice *ideomotor* (unconscious body-movement) signs, including those above, but not *ideosensory* (unconscious body-sensation) signs, in which the client experiences the switch to unconscious communication without showing any behavioral indications that the practitioner can see. For example, the practitioner may tell a client, "Your arms are very light," and the client may feel that lightness but not raise her arms. The practitioner cannot see any indication of her sensation of lightness. There may be many times, therefore, when a client is in hypnosis, but it is not detected by the practitioner. The bottom line is that hypnosis is a natural state, one we find ourselves in many times each day. Highway hypnosis, zoning out, daydreaming, and that creative flow state are all hypnotic states. We go through a *hypnogogic* state on the way to sleep and a *hypnopompic* state as we wake up; at these times—not fully awake and not fully asleep—we are in that altered mental state of hypnosis.

There is no such thing as someone who cannot be hypnotized, because our brains put us in that state often without our even knowing it. Someone may be disinclined to go into hypnosis on demand in a practitioner's office, however. And this supports the assumption that some people are not suggestible or hypnotizable. Thinking this way, to me, is counterproductive, as it reinforces the impression that hypnosis is some kind of special ability that some people have and others do not. Or perhaps a magical process that you either believe in or not. *In reality, saying you don't believe in hypnosis is like saying you don't believe in gravity.* It exists, regardless.

But belief is a powerful force and can impact how easily someone goes into hypnosis during a session, or whether they go into it at all. As Henry Ford famously said, "Whether you believe you can or believe you can't, you're right."

Hypnosis is not easy—it's perhaps impossible—to define as a distinct state of consciousness, however. It's not necessary, either, and may actually be a shift of communication processes from left- to right-brain dominance. Preceding hypnosis, the conscious mind is in control, whereas in the latter situation, unconscious processes dominate. Seeing hypnosis as a process rather than as a state helps us understand why there can be such different responses from people in it, including hypnotic coma, convulsive states, catharsis, relaxation, etc. Moreover, different suggestions and protocols make the experience of hypnosis different. Many people don't notice any change in how they feel, yet therapeutic changes still occur.

A hundred years ago it was thought there was no hypnosis without a long induction, but this is no longer credited as true. Stage hypnotist Dave Elman made a name for himself by teaching therapists how to do rapid inductions in order to spend more session time on therapy rather than taking up half the session getting the client to access his unconscious mind.[23] We often use instant inductions now. One effective method is to have the client focus on an image or body sensation, which can immediately silence the inner voice, switching communication to unconscious processes. Even getting in touch with a deep issue or feeling can be labeled "rapid induction," as it is evidence of unconscious communication.

Hypnosis therefore does not deserve the condemnation of just drooling on yourself in a recliner. It does not require an induction, as hypnosis researchers have always assumed. To be at our most productive, creative, performing our best, and thinking most clearly, we instinctively activate that process of shifting to unconscious communication. This process allows us to *feel* whether something is right for us, whether it resonates with us, because conscious communication with our rational mind is turned down or off. *We don't always know when we're in hypnosis* because it's a natural way of letting unconscious, more automatic processes dominate brain activity in those moments.

And though this shift itself is largely unconscious, we can train ourselves to have control over it to some extent, just like we can with our heart rate.

The use of ritual, for example, can set up our brains for the shift from conscious to unconscious communication processes. We see this with athletes and performers, in particular, but anyone can use ritual to make that shift. A tennis player may start a ritual when he walks onto the court and up to the serving line. He stands in a particular location, feet in the same position every time. He shifts his weight from front foot to back foot and repeats this action three times—no more, no less. He touches the ball to a particular point on his racquet and then bounces the ball exactly three times, then touches the ball to his racquet again and lines up his shot. He's practiced the movement up to the serve many, many times, and it's automatic and perfect just so long as his rational, conscious mind stays out of the picture. The unconscious processes are in complete control, giving him the best possible outcome. He can feel any issues during the serve which create prediction error and cause his brain to reconstruct his serve program slightly to have an even better outcome next time. Is he "in hypnosis" during this activity? I would argue that yes, he is. The preceding ritual can be seen as a kind of induction.

Athletes aren't the only ones who benefit from ritual. Having a ritual prior to going into a business meeting or working on a project or doing anything at all is merely a way to shift internal communication for greater clarity of thought and emotional control. It's a good way to create a mindful state, to bring the body (and therefore mind) into better balance, which aids memory retrieval, effective interpersonal communication, and understanding. I have a quick way to make my head a blank slate; I tell myself to *shut up and listen*. When I stop trying to talk to myself and direct what's going on in my head and just listen for any images or feelings, being mindful, I feel that communication switch flip.

In sum, hypnosis is merely evidence of unconscious communication happening in the client, so anything producing emotional distance can be seen as tapping into this process. For example, an NLP technique that enables unconscious communication can be said to engage the hypnotic process with no induction necessary, though an induction may be helpful sometimes.

Modern hypnosis researchers distinguish between *trance* (which is the result of induction) and *suggestion* (which influences a client to think and feel differently about memories and concepts). But hypnotherapy is largely about gathering information. It's a way to flip the switch to unconscious communication to hear what the unconscious mind thinks is important. To change associations in the brain, this information gathering has to happen prior to any hypnotic suggestions or NLP techniques. Trying to give suggestions to change a behavior won't work if the behavior is not the issue but rather just a manifestation of the issue. We have to find out what the issue really is and change that, at which point any physical and psychological results of that issue go away.

Though we generally credit Franz Anton Mesmer for having created the first protocols that would eventually develop into modern hypnotherapy techniques, the origins of hypnosis extend at least as far back as the ancient Greek healing temples of Asclepius, where sleeping patients dreamed and when they woke interpreted their experiences as the gods speaking to them with healing suggestions, which were then sometimes backed up by the temple priests. Its more recent history, however, begins with Mesmer, an eighteenth-century physician working first in Austria and later in France, who contended that disease was caused by imbalances in a physical force, called *animal magnetism*, affecting various parts of the body. In this, he was following speculations by Newton about the effects of gravity on the body. Accordingly, Mesmer thought that cures could be achieved by redistributing some theorized magnetic fluid, a procedure that typically resulted in pseudoepileptic seizures known as "crises."

Mesmer's techniques, theories, and cures were very controversial, and in 1784 Louis XVI appointed not one but two Royal Commissions to investigate him. While working in Austria in 1775, Mesmer himself had conducted just such an investigation of Johann Gassner, a famous priest-exorcist, arguing that his cures were genuine but mediated by animal magnetism rather than the expulsion of evil spirits. Later, in Paris, Mesmer repeatedly called for a similar investigation of his own claims.[24]

As with Gassner, Mesmer's techniques were eventually discredited as a result of objective external investigation—but his cures were accepted as bona fide. The investigators determined that he got results, as claimed, but not from animal magnetism.

The truth is that I have never hypnotized anyone but myself. Nobody has. Hypnosis is not voodoo or magic. It is a natural, unconscious brain process. Coming from this perspective, hypnosis can only ever be self-hypnosis. A practitioner can use some influential words and/or actions, but she cannot control the client's mind. She can also use some brain hacks to help the client reconstruct a memory or reprogram a feeling, but she is not the agent of change; the client is.

Consequently, we refer to hypnotherapy as a *co-creative process*. The practitioner is like the mountain climber's sherpa. She has the map and the client's bags on her llama, but the client decides where to go and has to hike alongside the sherpa to get there.

But the most common misconception people have about hypnosis is that it is something done *to* them, not *by* them. This is just one of many misconceptions. I recall how a client was interested in hypnotherapy, but the head of her church had warned her sternly that it was evil, that it opened the mind for the devil to get in. Now she is one of my most ardent supporters and helps to correct others' misconceptions.

The best story I have of a prospective client coming in with a misconception about hypnotherapy is the woman who said her neighbor was a witch who put a spell on her and she needed me to take it off.

Don't even get me started on how hypnosis is portrayed in movies and on television.

Because of these misunderstandings, I first educate all my clients on what hypnotherapy is and answer any questions they may have about it.

One thing I do not do, however, is test them for suggestibility. As mentioned previously, there are big individual differences in how suggestible, or hypnotizable, someone is on demand using formal hypnotic techniques. But this does not mean that everyone cannot achieve that state on demand. It just might take some of them more time and perhaps a bit of coaching or preparatory homework. Additionally, there are many different practitioners with different styles, some of whom will resonate with a client and some of whom won't, which greatly impacts the client's results and even whether the client will go into a hypnotic state in the office.

I, myself, had a related negative experience recently. I downloaded a really nice hypnosis app onto my phone and was excited to use it. The first thing it had me do was take a suggestibility test, during which the practitioner led me through an induction and a series of tests to determine whether I was in a hypnotic state. I failed miserably, scoring a 1 out of 10. The app wouldn't let me use any of the tools in it but invited me to come back and retest at a later time. For the record, I can go into a hypnotic state instantly whenever I want to. I just didn't resonate with the style of person giving the test. This experience made me wonder how many people have turned their backs on hypnotherapy based on concluding or being told they cannot be hypnotized.

Many physical and mental health practitioners understand its benefits, but many others do not and therefore do not make their patients aware that this option exists. Add to this the extensive misconceptions and the suggestibility tests, and it seems likely that many people who might be helped are not trying it because they don't see it as a viable solution. This is unfortunate, especially considering that modern hypnotherapy was borne of the medical profession over a century ago *and has been taught in medical schools ever since.*

A valid concern about hypnotherapy is the accuracy of a client's memories. Several decades ago, the issue of implanted memories surfaced as a real problem for some people. Psychotherapists were using hypnosis in a way that led their patients to believe horrible things about their past that were untrue. Such was the power of suggestion. For example, a patient was asked under hypnosis to remember a time when her father molested her. Though the intentions of these therapists were undoubtedly positive, this approach of feeding suggestions to the client had grossly negative consequences. They were leading the witness, something that *is not done in hypnotherapy.*

Hypnotherapists do not diagnose or treat any illnesses or clinical disorders. Those of us who do anything other than read a canned script to our clients use coaching techniques. Coaches by definition don't hand out advice or lead the client in any direction; they help the client come to his own understanding about himself and figure out what changes he wants to make, if any. Because we don't have a treatment plan for the client, we don't have an agenda that can influence the session. Whatever comes up from the client's brain, whether it seems to make sense or not, is what we go with. In fact, many of the most revealing sessions I've had with my clients were initiated by some crazy ideas or images, like the man who finally understood why he could not control some of his habits by following a knowledgeable guardian angel in the form of a giant cherry to a healing river.

Having no plan or agenda allows us to have sessions with clients without even knowing what the sessions are about. A young lady in high school came in with her mother one day, wanting help with her fear of returning to school. Something happened there that scared her at a deep enough level that she couldn't bring herself to return. When I asked if she could tell me what happened, she immediately shook her head no. Then I asked if she could see a small part of the scary event playing like a little mental movie in her head; she nodded. *Without ever knowing what the event was,* I led her through a protocol to release that fear. She left, feeling better, able to go back to school. I couldn't have influenced her, even if I had wanted to, as I didn't even know what was going on. I didn't need to, because she, not I, was the one reconstructing that memory.

The unconscious mind talks to us in images and loves symbolism, so sessions are often amusing—fun for adults and children alike. I've had some young clients with big issues who don't want to see another doctor or talk to another stranger about their problems. Some also really want to solve their problems themselves. When I teach them about their unconscious superpower and let their brains write the story that becomes our session, they not only feel more comfortable and happier, but they also feel more powerful and confident.

I particularly remember one little guy who wet his pants at school, as well as when he slept, which was very embarrassing. Added to that, making his confidence even lower, his older brother constantly attempted to control him. As he didn't want me to know that he wet his pants, we worked on his self-confidence. I had him conjure an imaginary village, and he immediately described one in Hawaii with a waterfall and a big guy in a house across from it. In the center of the village a statue of a man stood proudly, his hand over his heart. I helped him associate a confident feeling with putting his own hand over his heart like the statue—an anchor he could use anytime he wanted to feel more confident. For a few sessions we built on his village imagery. Meanwhile, he no longer wet his pants. His mom reported one exception when he wet his bed after about two weeks because he stood up to his brother that day for the first time ever and made him cry. He felt so bad that he wet the bed that night. Then he got over it and kept standing up for himself with no further issues.

These unconsciously directed sessions allow the client to communicate with herself in perhaps a different way than she is used to, listening to and acting on images, emotions, and body sensations instead of that inner voice that's babbling at her all day long, often counterproductively making her feel bad. Learning to communicate like this with herself, she has an easier time understanding what is right for her and what is not. Even decision-making is easier and more accurate with no more buyer's remorse, unlike when the decisions are made based on verbal reasoning.

One of my clients told me that she had never made a decision in her entire life that she had not regretted. I had her start visualizing alternatives and scanning her body for any discomfort. Whichever alternative left her feeling relaxed was the right one. She practiced this technique on a family vacation, during which she wanted to buy a handbag as a souvenir of her trip. Every bag she picked up, she closed her eyes and visualized herself using it. Scanning her body, she noted if there was any negative sensation anywhere. If there was, then something about that bag didn't work for her. She said that she knew instantly which bag was the right one and for the first time felt really good about her decision.

Did she go into a hypnotic state for a moment while she visualized each bag? If we define hypnosis as the switch point from conscious to unconscious communication processes, then yes, she did, and instantly.

There are several situations in which our brains naturally put us into a hypnotic state, and we hypnotherapists capitalize on this. When we're bored, we will zone out—our minds tend to drift off into a hypnotic state. When we're startled by, say, a loud noise, our brains go offline for a moment, and in that instant we are very suggestible, as we unconsciously open ourselves up to any information about what caused the startling event. Similarly, when we're overwhelmed, we feel like we just can't think, can't cram one more bit of information into our heads, and we mentally check out. All hypnotherapy inductions use one or more of these situations. For example, we may lead a client to mentally walk down a quiet pathway until he is bored and goes into hypnosis. We may startle a client with a hand clap and immediately instruct him to close his eyes and rest. Or we may overwhelm a client into hypnosis by having her keep staring at our left eye while she pushes her hand against ours with increasing pressure and simultaneously feels her body sink down into her chair. We don't perform magic spells; we just take advantage of how the brain naturally works. We work with your brain, not against it, and teach you how you can too.

We know that there are successive levels of hypnosis, from light to deep. For light hypnosis, perhaps just focusing on images while silencing that inner voice is all that is required. That wouldn't be sufficient for deeper hypnosis-induced brain changes. It is fine for suggestion therapy, but somnambulism or hypnotic coma may be necessary if you want to use self-hypnosis for anesthesia during surgery, for example. When people practice going into a hypnotic state, changing how they communicate with themselves, using whatever technique works best for them, they can get really good at it really fast and flip that switch instantly on demand. As opposed to bringing their mind back to a focal point like we do with meditation, they can let their mind wander, getting information from their unconscious mind about what is important for them to address. They can make changes in how they think, feel, and behave. They can also just enjoy having some deep relaxation time.

Chapter Seven

Benefits of Hypnotherapy and Related Protocols

OVER THE YEARS, OVER a thousand people have met with me for consultations to learn more about hypnotherapy and its benefits. Considering all the misinformation out there, I understood their skepticism. One objection to it is that it is pseudoscientific, a claim made until very recently by Wikipedia, everyone's favorite online encyclopedia. This is incorrect but has been corrected, which makes me very happy. Hypnotism, in fact, has the endorsement of the Mayo Clinic.

A large amount of empirical research, in the past and continuing today, shows both psychological and physical advantages of hypnotherapy either in lieu of or in addition to medical and psychological protocols. The more research done, the more credibility it receives.

Benefits typical for all clients regardless of issue include increased relaxation, physical and emotional comfort, and better-quality sleep. Research shows greater reduction of symptoms, higher quality-of-life estimates, and fewer signs of depression and anxiety[25]; less pain (acute and chronic), fatigue, and nausea; less need for medication, as well as less time in the operating room, fewer side effects, less anticipatory anxiety, easier adherence to doctors' treatment plans, and increased ability to overcome emotional and physical limitations to achieve therapeutic closure.[26] These effects have been demonstrated in a wide variety of physical and mental health conditions. Many studies show that patients who add hypnotherapy to their recovery regimen spend less time in the hospital, leaving up to three days earlier than those who do not.[27] It allows the brain to focus on healing more than it otherwise would, resulting in faster recovery. Two meta-analyses that included seventy-six studies confirmed many of the above-mentioned benefits, as well as finding evidence that cancer symptoms were effectively controlled with hypnosis.[28]

One of my clients—we'll call him Paul—perfectly exemplified how hypnotherapy can lower blood pressure. Very dedicated to his health and one of the fittest people I've ever met, he came in for his consultation exasperated and frustrated because his blood pressure had been in the high range for five years, and nothing he or his doctor did had moved the needle. After a session to reduce his stress level, I gave him a self-hypnosis exercise to do at home.

Paul was nothing if not disciplined and serious about making this change; in fact, he spent so much time doing that exercise that his wife started to worry. "Are you sure you're not doing that too much?" she asked him after noticing that he was spending all of his free time sitting silently with his eyes closed.

"Amy told me to do this as much as possible," he told her as she looked at him warily, then dropped the subject.

A week later he had an appointment with his doctor; right off, he got a blood pressure reading. Then another one. And a third one. All of these readings showed his blood pressure on the low side of normal, a shift so unusual and dramatic that the doctor and technicians were concerned the machine was broken. They took another reading on his way out—same low numbers.

He also noticed that according to the fitness monitor he wore on his wrist, he was no longer waking up twelve to thirteen times per night, as he had been since starting to track it. Now he was waking up two to three times.

Another client likewise had a very drastic physical change following a single session of hypnotherapy. Diagnosed with stage-three cirrhosis, she'd been unable to improve that situation, even while seeing five health care practitioners, some traditional and some alternative, over the course of two years. In our first session we discovered a fear that directly impacted her, and we got rid of it. I also had her add a chicken breast to her daily diet because she was eating almost no protein. A week and a half later she sent me an email: "I just got back from an appointment with my primary doctor, and she's doing cartwheels because my lab results have reversed and are looking better for the first time in years!" Was this improvement because of the hypnotherapy or the chicken? Probably both. Poor nutrition is a physical stressor that impacts both physical and mental health. Reducing her stress by releasing her fear also helped her both psychologically and physically.

Research shows that hypnotherapy affords benefits beyond relaxation, meditation, cognitive-behavioral therapy, psychoanalysis, and medication, and *it does so faster and in a way that can be easier emotionally on patients*. For example, hypnotic analgesia (reduced sensitivity to pain) has been found superior to morphine, diazepam, aspirin, acupuncture, and biofeedback, and it relieves both physical pain and psychological suffering.[29]

As I like to emphasize, unlike drugs and psychotherapy, there are really only positive side effects of hypnotherapy and related unconscious interventions. This is the reason there is no licensure required or even available for hypnotherapy. No government is going to spend time and money on a licensing board for a service in which "I wanted a refund and didn't get one" is the biggest complaint it gets. I believe the explanation is that this group of techniques enables the brain to make only changes that positively impact the body budget. This contrasts with trying to force a change using conscious or biochemical means and then determining if that change was beneficial or detrimental to the body budget. Sometimes such changes, beneficial in some ways, can be harmful in others, and the net effect may not be positive. The worst thing that can happen using unconscious, client-directed strategies, by contrast, is a zero-sum change.

At times when we see what appears to be a negative change, in my experience it signals a deeper issue. Resolve that issue, reprogram it, and the resulting change is positive. It's like finding a land mine that needs to be cleared. One of my first cases illustrates this idea well. She came in for help sleeping—often a quick fix. A little work with hypnotic suggestions, and most poor sleepers are good to go. We had a great first session, which ended with her yawning so much that she was questioning whether she would even make it home without falling asleep. I gave her a little self-hypnosis exercise to do to reinforce the brain changes we made, and she was on her way.

The next morning I received a long email, informing me she'd had the worst night's sleep ever! Should she continue sessions? she wondered. I suggested that she stop doing the exercise I gave her and just focus on breathing and telling herself she was okay. At her next session, with her brain primed for digging deeper, we investigated that feeling she got when she tried to sleep but couldn't. What emerged out of that session was her guilt for not being able to spend more time taking care of her ailing father. She felt like a bad daughter. Anguished over this, she couldn't function during the day, so she put it in a mental closet. It nagged at her unconsciously during the night. When we gave her brain the suggestion that she slept well at night, it had a freak-out, bereft of its coping mechanism. In the following two sessions I helped her get rid of the feeling of guilt, and she's been sleeping well ever since.

Sleep is one of many areas in which a solution such as hypnotherapy has an advantage over medication. Sleep medication, both prescription and over the counter, may help a patient fall asleep more quickly and sleep longer, but it impairs the quality of sleep, creating a different type of disorder, called *iatrogenic*, or medically induced. No such side effects occur with hypnotherapy intervention. Such unconscious-oriented strategies in our toolbox can help us increase healing and improve our quality of life, and we can use them alone or in conjunction with other types of strategies.

Many people consider hypnotherapy to be an alternative to medical or psychotherapy treatment. I am not always of that view, but many who hold that view come into my office. They have lost faith in the medical system or the mental health system, or they don't want invasive and potentially harmful treatments. I get it. I have had disappointing experiences with our medical system too, but I'm very glad it's there when I need it. I'm glad it's there for my clients as well.

I consider what I do to be more complementary than alternative to medical and psychotherapy interventions. If someone comes into my office with physical symptoms, I make sure they get them checked out by an appropriate doctor prior to addressing them. If there is a physical cause, then they will need a physical solution. Hypnotherapy can precipitate physical changes by clearing up the psychological cause of an issue or by keeping the issue from the person's awareness – which may or may not be a good thing. Pain, for example, is an alerting signal letting you know that you need to stop what you're doing to avoid physical damage. Deleting this signal if there is damage being done will result in more damage.

Hypnotherapy reduces pain not via the opioid system, as the resulting changes cannot be reversed by giving the patient Narcan, as happens with opioid medications; rather, it may prevent pain from reaching conscious awareness by restructuring brain connections. It is quite clear from the last two decades of research that hypnosis impacts pain perception to the level of surgical anesthesia by enabling the modification of many areas of the brain, from the prefrontal cortex, which modulates emotion, to the Default Mode Network to areas specific to pain perception. It even controls cardiovascular responses to painful stimuli, keeping the patient calm.[30]

One of my colleagues, facing back surgery, chose to replace anesthesia with hypnosis, which has been a documented use for hypnosis since the nineteenth century and is still used today. It's not used very often, though, and she received a lot of pushback from the hospital staff. This is understandable, as they can't have patients wasting time messing around with techniques that may ultimately not work and negatively impact the surgery. But I was amazed at the hostility she encountered from a pre-op nurse, who kept offering her chemical anesthesia to no avail. The nurse was shouting at her, making such a ruckus that the surgeon came in to ask what the matter was. My colleague explained that she was a hypnotherapist and wanted to put herself under for surgery. He said he wanted to watch that and walked with her into the operating room.

As she got into position on the operating table, the surgeon told her to take her time. Flipping her internal communication switch, she went to her mental island, and when she started drinking her favorite tropical drink, she gave him a thumbs-up. He made a tiny cut into her back and looked around at her face. She seemed fine, so he kept cutting. Looking at her again, he asked, "How are you doing?" She gave him another thumbs-up. About halfway through the operation, he smacked his hand on the operating table and said, "I'm so proud of you!" These techniques are so robust that neither a smack on the table nor a cut into her back made her feel any pain.

When the surgery was complete, she walked out of the room with no need for the typical post-operative recovery. She took a wheelchair to the hospital entrance (not allowed to walk there for legal reasons), where she got up, walked to her car, and went home. Because her brain expected not to feel any pain, she never had any.

Pain, as I have said, is an alerting mechanism that can be dangerous to remove. With medication, that entire mechanism is removed, and we can actually do more damage to our bodies, as we no longer have the pain alert. With hypnotherapy, in contrast, we can silence pain while adding an alerting sensation, such as a mild tingling if the area of discomfort changes negatively; in that case, a doctor should take a look. Drugs have no such failsafe. Right after having his ankle rebuilt, a man came to me because he couldn't stand the way he felt on the opiate pain medication he was prescribed, so he stopped taking it and was in terrible postoperative pain. We had one hypnotherapy session, in which I taught him how to modulate his pain using his brain; he came back into consciousness completely comfortable. When he put his feet down after relaxing in the recliner, he had a brief jolt of discomfort as the blood rushed to his feet, which almost immediately turned into a slight tingle. Wide eyed and with a growing smile, he looked at me and said, "That is so cool!" To keep his brain focused on healing his ankle, I made a custom recording for him. And—with no medication—he recovered quickly.

It's my belief that a patient has a responsibility to do whatever he can to improve and maintain his own health. He works with doctors and other medical professionals toward this goal. People often have the mindset, though, that the doctor alone is responsible. By tapping into his body's natural healing system, hypnotherapy helps the patient do his part of this job, and I would like to see more referrals by the medical profession to hypnotherapists to help equal out this part of this equation.

Some medical providers are clued into the value of hypnotherapy, and they are quick to support its inclusion in their patients' treatment. I had a longtime client, a nurse, with multiple major health issues. Having undergone many surgeries, all at the hospital where she worked, she knew the staff very well, and they knew her.

When she went to a checkup with her doctor prior to having her thyroid removed, her doctor threatened to cancel her surgery. He was worried about her because she was acting abnormally for her. She was too relaxed, he said.

He asked her what was up, and she told him that to prepare for surgery, she was seeing a hypnotherapist. He asked who, and she told him my name. He said that several of his patients had seen me, with positive results. He told her the surgery was back on and to keep seeing me and doing what I told her to. She sailed through the surgery, needing no meds afterwards for pain or even for nausea, which had always been a big problem for her—amazing her doctor by how fast she recovered. For a hip replacement at a later date she used the same strategy, with the same results.

That client met me for lunch one day, bringing along a friend, a nurse administrator at a major hospital system. As we chatted at the table, waiting for our order, my client mentioned that she had a headache. Her friend immediately started digging into the mobile pharmacy that was her purse, but my client told her not to bother. Her friend watched as my client closed her eyes for a few moments, then opened them, smiled, and said "Ah, that's better. All gone." Her friend turned to me. "I'm going to need your business card," she said.

Hypnotherapy helps patients at all points along the time course from first finding a medical problem to completely recovering from it. Several years ago, a mother brought her teenage boy in for help prepping for surgery. He had just recently been told he needed to have his thyroid removed. Mom was scared for her son, but he was very easy-going, trying to be brave and keep his mom calm.

The first thing we did was get rid of the fight-or-flight body response that he still felt from finding the lump a year prior when he saw his throat in his bathroom mirror. Then we got rid of anticipatory anxiety about the surgery, and I taught him how to manage any discomfort.

Mom said that on their drive to the hospital she kept trying to reassure him, but he kept telling her to be quiet so he could do the exercise I'd taught him. She let him do his thing, and he went into surgery relaxed and happy. She got the pain-pill prescription filled so that when he woke up he could start taking the medication, but he wasn't interested. He told her he was fine without meds. Mom sent me a picture of him, sitting up cross-legged in the hospital bed, texting his brother like it was any other day; only, he had a big bandage on his neck. He never took any of the pills. And his mom noticed, as a side benefit, an increase in his self-confidence.

These are not isolated instances. There are many stories like this. Hypnotherapy can be of significant value to patients and doctors to minimize the negative impacts of medical interventions while allowing patients to get the value that the medical world has to offer. It's a win-win.

This symbiotic relationship exists with other mental-health interventions, as well. Some people don't want to, or feel they cannot, talk about their problems. A therapist has a difficult time coming up with a treatment plan for someone who won't talk much or at all. But that is not a problem for practitioners of these unconscious-directed approaches. There are people who want to be in control of their own healing, and with hypnotherapy the client is in complete control. Throughout the entire session, we take what the clients say at face value and help them come to their own conclusions by helping them listen to unconscious processes that are not always available for us to hear consciously. We do not view our clients' issues through a lens of diagnosis and treatment.

Listening to the unconscious directly, free of the filtering mechanisms that allow only certain information into consciousness for rational thought, can allow a dismissed part of the client to be heard, perhaps for the first time. One of my clients had always been very stressed out by social interactions, especially with family members. She seemed always scared and tired. When I had her get in touch with the part of her mind that was making her feel that way, she discovered a little girl constantly screaming into a black hole; nobody heard that child, who, having been repeatedly sexually abused by family and others, was trying to protect herself but was not able to get anyone to listen and help, which made her feel helpless and guilty.

She admitted it, crying. After thanking this inner child for doing all she could to help the client, I asked her what she wanted, now that those days of sexual abuse were over. She said that she just wanted to be a kid, to be able to trust herself and others, and to feel nurtured. I helped her reconstruct some relevant concepts that had been maladaptively constructed in the first place, after which she has noticed an improvement in her arousal and affect.

We let the unconscious be heard, resolving a long-term issue by allowing that part of the client to fully process it and reprogram her brain to positively influence her body budget.

Unconscious strategies such as hypnotherapy help eliminate *secondary gains* for clients, as well. These clients hold on to their issues because they are getting something of value from them.

It seems counterintuitive for someone to want to keep a problem in their life, but it is actually quite common. One client came to me after being fired as a patient by multiple doctors because she kept wanting them to diagnose her with illnesses they found no evidence of. She had a terrible view of the medical establishment, seeing it as inept, as she had real symptoms, which kept changing, for which they had no solutions. When she and I investigated her symptoms, she learned from her unconscious mind that the only time she felt love and caring from her husband was when she had a medical issue. These issues started with a very real battle with cancer, which she beat, but continued due to her secondary gain of having gotten affection from her husband when she was sick.

We often use secondary gains to bond with people we either never had as good a relationship with as we wanted or had a great relationship with and lost, like another of my clients. This man had a wonderful relationship with his father, who had passed away five years prior. He came to me for back pain, which continued even after surgery. His father had suffered from the same pain and had the same surgery. I had him talk to his pain, and it told him that it wasn't real. After he returned to full consciousness, I asked him if he thought he might be trying to bond with his father with that shared pain. "I don't know," he said. "But that's an interesting idea."

I had him come up with a more positive way to bond with him—through their shared sense of humor. After that, he no longer needed the marijuana his doctor had prescribed him for pain and suffering.

When we do all we can to promote our innate healing processes, we need less external help. Getting bladder control back in a couple of weeks using a hypnosis recording keeps many people from having to expend a much greater amount of time, money, and discomfort with medications and surgery that, in many cases, have a less-than-stellar success rate and may cause more trouble down the road. We can make sure we're in the best possible situation, with the best possible impact on our body budget, to heal as quickly and completely as possible, whether or not physical interventions are necessary. It's how we can do our part, and it's an ultimate goal of all brain activity.

Chapter Eight

Outcomes of an Unconscious-Oriented Approach

ACCEPTING THE ASSUMPTION THAT *our brains have evolved to change our programming to work toward body-budget balancing*, we get a different view of maladaptive constructions and reconstructions that our brains have developed over the years. Seeing ourselves as broken or at war with ourselves is incorrect and unhelpful. Instead, it may be more correct to see any maladaptive programming as *having served us at some time*, after which the program just kept running; that is, it wasn't always maladaptive. It is an indication that issues that caused that programming are still there, negatively impacting us. They have to go, and if we listen to that unconscious part of the brain that is concerned with letting go of anything that throws off our body budget, we can discover and change these problematic programs. The key is to see the negative stress and emotions that result from this programming as informational, not punishing. Those physical signs and feelings are ultimately positive, letting us know what we can do to improve our lives.

Changing our focus from listening to the inner voice of our conscious minds to listening to our unconscious minds that inform us via images, emotions, and body sensations allows us to get more accurate information about what our issues are. It gives us the ability to immediately and easily reduce how aroused we get by them and improving the affect attached to them. We can sometimes change the affect from negative to positive. But for deeper causes or more debilitating programming, we do not achieve a positive affect; rather, in these situations, we see interoceptive information change from negative to neutral. An event so difficult it produces dissociation—shoving a memory deep underneath more superficial awareness—likely does not have enough of a silver lining to ever be experienced as positive. But you can achieve emotional distance, reprogramming the event to feel neutral and allowing the brain to take resolution of it off of its "to do" list.

Just as some filtering and selection mechanisms actively make certain information in the brain available to our inner voice, there are others that allow certain information to come up from the vast archives of our unconscious mind when we *silence* that voice and *just listen* to the images, emotions, and body sensations that arise into our awareness. Successfully processing an issue this way is like cleaning a layer of scum from the top of a pond. It looks and feels great until another issue that couldn't reach the surface before starts to bubble up and we become aware of its negative influence on our body budget. We see this as information from the unconscious about something else we can change to improve our lives, and we are able to focus on clearing that, too, off the pond. We keep going until nothing else bubbles to the surface.

Using these unconsciously directed sessions, I start with more superficial issues, such as unwanted habits or self-sabotage, and allow the client's unconscious to lead us to the deeper causes. We keep working on the deeper, more core issues, such as confidence or a sense of worthiness, until the brain presents us with another superficial issue. That's when we know we have cleared all of the deeper issues the client's brain deems appropriate at the time.

For example, I worked with an older client on aftereffects—in the form of negative body-budget changes—from molestation when she was young, which had resulted in a feeling of unworthiness in all areas of her life. One day she came in saying, "I've got a burrito supreme problem. I can't go a single day without getting a burrito supreme from Taco Bell." That was the biggest thing on her mind. She had cleared the bigger influences in her body budget and was now focused on clearing up more superficial ones. A couple of weeks later I saw her, and she said, "I have a bone to pick with you. I want to go to Taco Bell every day but can't bring myself to." She laughed and said that she really didn't care about going there anymore and was feeling, overall, much better.

We know that brain-programming changes made with these kinds of approaches positively impact our body budget because changing one issue for the better results in *everything* feeling better, even situations completely unrelated to the reprogramming. Because they aren't as stressful or emotionally difficult to address as they used to be, these changes also make it easier to get to deeper issues. So we start chipping away at more superficial manifestations of an issue, organically follow the brain deeper to avoid freak-outs, and then clean up any remaining superficial difficulties or annoyances that remain. This process may take a few sessions or many years, with some sessions producing immediate, drastic change, like a switch flipping, and others taking more time to chip away at until the issue collapses and the client is filled with a great sense of lightness and freedom.

The life changes I have seen throughout the course of working with deeper issues over longer periods of time have been profound. Living more unconsciously by relying less on conscious interpretation of interoceptive information (avoiding the middleman) results in a reconstruction of our self-concept and greater *awareness of that reconstruction*. We gain a better understanding of what information and experiences resonate with us, or feel right, leading to a more positive impact on our body budget. We therefore switch our identity from the conscious inner voice to a feeling-based part of our unconscious that is closely tied to our self-concept. Instead of relying on rational thought to tell us what is best for us, based on its interpretation of the bits and pieces of information it receives from our self-referent processes, we more directly access—by listening to images, emotions and body sensations—the part of our unconscious that informs us of who we are and what we really want and need. What resonates with us taps into the representation of self in the brain and the processes that utilize it to think, feel, and behave in ways that improve our body budget. Allowing a healthy self-concept to direct our decisions reduces self-doubt and increases productivity, creativity, and happiness.

When you ask an unconscious part of the brain why it keeps trying to sabotage a client's self-care or her attempts to create the life she wants, the answer always boils down to *keeping her as happy as possible by protecting her from situations which, based on past experiences, are likely to make her feel bad*. When we give that part the new job of making her feel, think, and act in ways that help make her happiness and wellbeing a top priority in her life, she feels more worthy and empowered and is a better role model for others who want to do the same. That positive influence, that good juju, is felt by family, friends, and potentially even strangers she passes on the street. She radiates more positive energy in her smile, her good deeds, and her appearance. One of my longtime clients noticed that over the years she spent cleaning up massive issues from an abusive childhood, her wardrobe changed from dark and neutral to brighter and more colorful, more in line with how much happier and more empowered she felt. In these ways she pays it forward, helping others make changes to improve their body budgets by being around her good energy; now she sets a good example of healthy living. We are a social species, and our brains are exquisitely sensitive to and changed by our interactions with others.

Our brains are always protecting us by reconstructing memories and concepts to improve our body budget. Sometimes, however, as in the examples in this book, these changes need reprogramming. A strategy that may seem like a good idea at the time, especially to a still-developing brain, may wind up being maladaptive. I had a mom bring her teenage son in for test anxiety, something I see very often that is almost always quickly and easily eliminated. He did well in school but just couldn't pass his driving test. It wasn't clear why. It didn't take long to realize that his issue was about something deeper; he was really scared of growing up and being out on his own. He'd seen older siblings and friends have trouble finding good jobs or they weren't able to afford apartments; he couldn't imagine that he'd do better. Unable to get a job because he couldn't drive, he stayed home, where he was taken care of by his mom.

His half-baked teenage brain saw the advantage of keeping him from being able to drive. It was telling him, "Don't go out there, because it's not going to end well. Stay home, where you're surviving just fine; your mother feeds you and does your laundry; otherwise, you'll wind up broke with ten crazy roommates and pink clothes and in danger of starving if your can opener breaks."

Your brain wants you to avoid anything that produces enough stress to negatively impact your body budget. You procrastinate doing something that makes you overly aroused, taking you out of balance, because avoiding it is your brain's way of keeping you from feeling bad.

That strategy doesn't make it feel any better in the long run, though; in fact, avoiding anything that creates discomfort tends to make the problem worse by strengthening the brain's repulsion response to it. In these situations, it can seem like we're at war with ourselves.

Hypnotherapy and other unconscious interventions focus on making direct changes in interoception, decreasing arousal from things that cause us too much stress and improving affect associated with events. Difficult tasks feel more doable, people-pleasing at our own expense seems stupid, and allowing others to treat us badly flies in the face of our newfound sense of worthiness. We no longer stress over decisions because to orchestrate brain activity that is right for us, we listen to and trust the brain processes tied to our self-concept, thus positively impacting our body budget. We sleep better, and things that used to cause overreactions are just not that big of a deal anymore.

Creative thinking, or innovative problem-solving, improves as well, because it necessitates unconscious direction and reliance. To quote Albert Einstein, "I don't write consciously—it is as if the muse sits on my shoulder." The famous Broadway playwright and screenwriter Neil Simon has said, "I slip into a state that is apart from reality." Rational mental activity, relying on slow, serial processing, only produces variations of past solutions; it's not a source of something new and different. After our conscious minds have thought about something to the point of giving up, we tend to feel frustrated, on the brink of failure at solving the problem. But in reality, our unconscious mind has determined that we've done all we can, and it is now time to let it take over and come up with something fabulous. This hand-off to purely unconscious processes is called *incubation*. We are not aware of our parallel unconscious problem-solving processes because they would overwhelm us, so we feel as if it's not really us that comes up with the solution.

Connecting and merging information from disparate sources does not require consciousness. In fact, limiting consciousness may actually improve information integration. Keep in mind, though, that you have to spend some time consciously thinking about the issue before handing it off to your unconscious for incubation. Why? Just like learning how to play the guitar, you have to understand as much as possible about the problem or project. Once you know what you need to know, backwards and forwards, inside and out, you can let your unconscious play.

After all, as Einstein famously said, "Creativity is just intelligence having fun." Perhaps this is why it has been so difficult, if not impossible, for researchers to tease apart the constructs of creativity and happiness. Indeed, Mihaly Csikszentmihalyi's work, culminating in his book *Flow: The Psychology of Optimal Experience*, convincingly argues that happiness comes from engaging in creative activity that challenges us to an optimal extent, not too easy and not too hard. This produces a state of what he termed *flow*, or more popularly referred to as being *in the zone* or *in the groove*, which is an unconscious, and I would argue hypnotic, state or process. We engage those self-referent processes tied to self-concept, bypassing the conscious, rational interpreter—at which point we no longer see ourselves as separate from the world around us or from the activity we are engaged in.[31]

This flow is the most productive state we can be in, as our unconscious, taking over, automatically engages and modifies cognitive and motor programs, as necessary, for optimal performance. Interoceptive changes from extensive practice put our body budget in the best possible place to successfully execute these programs. I've had many creatively blocked clients who got hung up second-guessing themselves at work or were not able to improve their musical or athletic performance because of some unconscious issue that was throwing off their body budget. Achieving more balance by reducing or eliminating the influence of those issues freed them from having their activities go to committee in their brains rather than being executed more automatically, as they should be after extensive experience has honed the accuracy of these processes.

Letting unconscious processes run without the conscious mind getting in the way results in an increase in clear, creative thinking, problem-solving, and performance. We get into the flow and work smarter, not harder. Expertly honed performance programs run optimally. We experience implicit concept reconstruction without explicit memory interference. Hypnotherapy may offer an advantage here, as it can dampen explicit memory without impacting implicit memory. We avoid the middleman, the interpreter, and go straight to the source, bypassing the pitfalls that can arise in interacting with our world when the conscious mind interferes.

When I was in college, a psychology class provided a great illustration of how my conscious mind could get in the way of unconscious reprogramming to mess up my interaction with the world. For about an hour I wore a pair of prism goggles, which flipped the world upside down, while a classmate led me around our college campus. During that time, my brain started reconstructing my visual reality. It was neuroplasticity in action. In that hour, whenever I tried consciously to determine where to place my feet—in going up stairs, for example—I made mistakes. But when I just moved in a way that felt right, without trying, I performed much better. Eventually, had I left the goggles on long enough, my vision would have flipped, making me see the world right side up—in spite of having the goggles on! Had I taken the goggles off at that point, I would have seen the world upside down—with no goggles on! But my brain would have quickly flipped it again to be normal.

Does our brain constantly reconstruct our "normal," as all of our concepts seem to get reconstructed by changes in arousal and affect from internal and external factors and experiences? Better relationships and interpersonal communication, both verbally and nonverbally, positively influence this reconstruction, which, in turn, positively influences our future interactions with others. As Linda Barrett has astutely commented, "It takes more than one human to create a human mind."[32]

We can directly improve the results of this reconstruction-interaction cycle by using unconscious-directed techniques such as hypnotherapy and NLP, which assist us in rewriting our life stories on demand and with intention, making whatever changes we choose in order to be the people we want to be. We can create ourselves and the lives we want to have.

Today people are really quick to try to find a pill to change how they feel, and many doctors are really quick to write prescriptions. Medication is almost always a doctor's first solution, to the point that many people think that doctors are overprescribing. I would have to agree, considering how many of my clients get off of medications. I had a young lady come in, taking three prescription sleeping meds at the same time! It only took a few sessions to get her doctor to take her off of two.

Another client, whom I have seen several times per month for a few years now, has greatly reduced or eliminated several psychoactive medications, including antipsychotics. As a child she spent time in a mental hospital and for sixty years felt that she had no control over her brain. This is no longer an issue for her. Now she has answers, some peace, and trust in herself and can successfully work through the recurrent early trauma that led to her brain being in that situation in the first place.

On the plus side, I think that our drug-centered culture recognizes that cognitive, emotional, and behavioral issues have a physical component. On the minus side, most people, including doctors, do not always see the mind and brain as two sides of the same coin. What happens to one affects the other. For some reason, we keep forgetting that psychological processes create chemical changes and those affect both mind and body. We also keep forgetting that the brain is part of the body.

Don't get me wrong; I'm not against medication. My experience with a clientele that largely is against taking medication has led me to believe that sometimes meds are necessary, and it's great that we have these options available. I just don't think such an invasive and potentially dangerous option should be our first resort to change brain programming, when a potentially better option exists to try first. If it doesn't work, take the meds and hopefully they will work. As I keep saying, *shouldn't our first resort be an option that only has positive side effects*, like increased feelings of confidence and empowerment?

We don't have to take a pill to change our brain chemistry. We can cause physiological change with psychological stimuli. In fact, pills only work, as I've pointed out, for the very reason that, using thoughts, feelings, and actions to change our brains, we are hard-wired to do the *same things for ourselves* that the pills do. Mind over matter is a thing.

Many people are adverse to stepping back from that conscious activity to try unconscious interventions, though. In fact, a significant number of participants, especially men, according to recent research, would rather endure electric shocks—which they previously said they would pay money to avoid—than be alone with their thoughts for as little as six minutes![33] Kind of explains why we're all on our mobile devices all the time rather than just gazing out a window for a while, huh? We feel we can control what we attend to better during a conscious web search than letting our unconscious tell us what we should focus on at the moment, which might not feel good. Even though we have so many pleasurable memories plus the ability to fantasize, which the lead author of those studies initially thought would make it easy and fun for his participants to entertain themselves in private, *they chose distraction*.

Letting our unconscious run the show can be scary because we are hard-wired to think more negative thoughts than positive and feel more negative feelings, no matter what part of the world we are from. We have more words for negative feelings, and we process them more deeply.[34] Add to that the indications that the right cerebral hemisphere is dominant during unconscious activity. That part of the brain's particular preoccupation with negative emotions makes it even more of a bummer—or does it?

If, as I contend, our brains are protecting us at all times, why would we be unconsciously focused more on negative thoughts and feelings than on feel-good ones? It stands to reason that if all of our thoughts and feelings were negative, we wouldn't even want to be alive, so that has no survival value. But if we were only focused on what's going right in our lives, we wouldn't see opportunities to change the things that aren't, which also has no survival value. Focusing mostly but not exclusively on negative thoughts and feelings provides us information and opportunities to keep making our lives better, which *does* have survival value.

This is where I think we need a perspective shift. Instead of believing that our minds bring up negative things to make us feel like our lives suck or that we have no control over our lives, we should understand that they're really trying to be constructive. This is an important distinction because the brain processes stressors differently than opportunities, with dissimilar downstream effects on our thoughts, feelings, and behaviors.

To see someone completely reprogram traumatic events, free themselves from their life-hindering repercussions in just a handful of hypnotherapy sessions, never ceases to amaze me. And I've come to realize, over the many years of doing this job, that even more amazing life transformations can accrue from regular sessions over time. In some of my clients who have made monthly or even bimonthly sessions a part of their ongoing self-care, I see incredible changes year after year. Their family and friends also notice these changes, and many of them wind up coming in for regular sessions, as well.

Hypnotherapy is a perfect first-choice intervention for so many people. It doesn't always work, but then nothing is 100 percent, including meds or therapy. Why not start with the fastest, easiest option that will at the very least help us reduce stress and increase success with other interventions, provided they are even necessary at that point? The ultimate goal of strategies that tap into our unconscious processes, bypassing rational thought, is to increase real control of our minds and bodies, to bring them into balance. This group of techniques—or brain hacks—works *with* our brains, not against them.

The objective of hypnotherapy and related techniques as *self-care* is to regularly reprogram negative feelings from past events, as well as from recent and even ongoing situations, and opening ourselves up to the opportunities those negative feelings help us to see. As clients reconstruct such events and release the negative feelings associated with them, they are free to grow in whatever direction makes them truly happy. With growth come new challenges, which may dredge up old fears and limiting beliefs that weren't significantly impacting them before but are now and need to be addressed. As the client continues to release negative programming, taking advantage of the opportunities that arise from them, and more quickly deal with new negative situations, she spends increased time in that rest-and-digest state of detoxification and clear thinking, and she is able to move her life creatively toward maximum joy and potential.

As I come to the end of our Seine River cruise, I can't help but reflect on how I've changed because of the experiences I've had over the last week, which have moved me closer to living my best life. When I first saw the amazing Eiffel Tower, I did not have to remind myself to remember it and the sense of awe I had every time I saw it. I'll never forget it. It is not a conscious, rational decision. I grew as an artist and person on this trip, and I will continue to see my world differently, more like Impressionist painters saw their world, because new perspectives have forever modified the information that comes in through my eyes. Previously held limiting beliefs are now, going forward, on my radar for active reprogramming.

My brain has changed for the better, improving future predictions of my world as I encountered even the slightest prediction error from interactions having to do with France and cruises and friends, because that's what it does. It's comforting to know that with each and every experience, whether we know it or not, our brains are constantly reconstructing our reality for maximum success in life and that there are things we can do to encourage our brains to rewrite our life stories the way we want them to impact us and help us grow—easy hacks to outsmart our brains when they are hung up. We reduce our stress, knowing that we have more control over our minds and bodies than we may have thought we had, because nobody told us.

So I'm telling you now.

Acknowledgements

This book has been decades in the making. It started germinating when I first learned about brain structure and function from the wonderful professors, researchers, and practitioners I was fortunate to work with, take classes from, and have discussions with at conferences and happy hours. Some I agreed with, others I didn't, but they all made me think more deeply and objectively about all areas of psychology, neuroscience, and philosophy, and I owe them all a debt of gratitude for feeding what became a beautiful lifetime obsession.

It wasn't until I had been doing hypnotherapy full time for a while that I felt I had added key elements to my education about how the brain works. For that I thank not only my trainers for getting me up and running in this arena, but also my clients and colleagues, from whose experiences and wisdom I continue to learn more every day. They forever changed my perspective on brain function.

As this book idea grew, it became painfully clear that knowing how to write professional journal articles did not make me a good writer of books. I owe some serious thanks to my writing coach, Brett Hilker, who provided structure and direction to help me get the manuscript written without getting lost in the weeds. That manuscript was turned into a readable book by my editor, Margaret Harrell, who helped me do more showing and less telling. She is the warm fuzziness to my cold scientific creepiness and is more than just an editor; she has become a writing mentor.

Last but nowhere near least, this book could not have bloomed without the support and encouragement of my family and friends, who certainly learned more than they ever wanted about the brain and hypnotherapy as I bounced ideas off of them and asked for feedback on early writing. I especially appreciated the strategic phone calls from my honey, Eric, my biggest supporter, and full-body hugs from my dog, Duke, to make sure I took breaks in my writing, making me pay attention to something else for a while and get back to my manuscript with fresh eyes; also helping keep my body budget in a decent place throughout the process. The celebratory words and wine from friends with each writing milestone achieved have without doubt been greatly appreciated.

What people are saying...

"I got into a serious auto accident a week ago . . . in a few sessions in the past week Dr. Amy took care of things that would have taken months on my own. I'm able to focus on getting better because I'm in control of my fears and my pain."

—Mike B.

"I recently had to have extensive dental work done, requiring hours in the dental chair. I prepped, using techniques Dr. Amy had taught me, and during the process each time I started stressing, I would hear her voice inside my head and I would use various calming techniques to center and relax myself. My dentist was very impressed!"

—Fran E.

"I can honestly say I no longer take any allergy medication, a huge improvement from taking Zyrtec daily."

—Bryan M.

"Thank you, Amy, for helping me to dig deeper & gain more access to my personal power."

—Preston C.

"i had never gone through anything like this so i really didn't know what to expect. i was pleasantly surprised when she did her thing and it actually worked on ME. AMAZING!!!!"

—John S.

"Dr. Rosner began with helping me get over my fear of snakes in one session, which then began an amazing journey for me to heal, grow, and become a better person."

—Monet S.

"Since I have been going to Amy, my life has greatly improved. I feel like a better version of myself. She gives you the tools to empower yourself to make lasting changes. She has taught me self-hypnosis practices I can do at home so that I may continue my own self-improvement. She can help with anything from seemingly minor life issues to past traumas."

— Sarah L.

"I'm not sure what you did but I had a different daughter this morning."

—Sherry L.

"Life changing."

—Jeanne K.

"A few years ago you helped my son when he was unable to eat, following a choking incident. I'm happy to report that he has never had the problem again after the one session with you."

—A. J.

"It helped me heal. And for the first time in years I have a real hope that life will one day return to normal."

—Colleen C.

"I just want to send a thank-you for all your help with my fear of getting on the airplane. I have taken three flights since our last session. So far so good."

—Jennifer S.

"My younger son had surgery in December to remove part of his thyroid. Prior to the surgery, I took him to see Amy to go over any fears he had about the procedure, the pain, etc. I couldn't be happier to report that he sailed through the surgery. and once we got home, he never once asked for pain medication. Added bonus—his demeanor has changed. He was always awesome, but now he's a little more confident, a little more self-possessed."

—D. J.

Also By Amy L. Rosner

Create Yourself: One-Month Journal

Use this journal to learn more about you, what makes you happy and what you may want to change—to create yourself. It is a mindfulness tool, a way to take note of the wonderful little things that happen every day that you may tend to overlook but that can lead to greater happiness. Most of all, it's a place to play and explore and have fun!

Create Yourself in Business: Use Your Own Unique Brand to Inspire Trust and Attract Ideal Clients

Create who you want to be in your business, not who you think you should be! Use all of the wonderful things about yourself—your style, your values, your personality, your passions, your dreams—to build your business from the ground up or change how you're currently doing things in your established business. Being you—unapologetically you—can help you attract your ideal clients and move from a lead follow-up numbers game to a referral-based business with the clients you really want to work with, who will be your raving fans. *Toss your advertising budget out the window and start inspiring yourself and others!*

A Year of Gratitude: 365-Day Journal

A gratitude journal can help you focus on the positives in your life, making you and those around you happier and increasing the odds of future successes. It's one thing to know you're grateful for something, but knowing why you're grateful for it takes it to another level, deepening your understanding and appreciation. This simple book provides a year of quick, easy journaling to make living in gratitude effortless. Inspirational quotes prompt you to see gratitude in new ways and in different aspects of your life every day. You never knew just how much you had in your life to be grateful for until now!

Thank You!

I HOPE YOU ENJOYED this book as much as I've enjoyed writing it! If you're so inclined, please leave a review on Amazon or wherever you purchased it. I would also welcome any direct communication at info@amyrosner.com.

Visit for more information about sessions, classes, books, and self-help products. For updates and helpful tidbits, follow me on Facebook, Instagram, LinkedIn, Pinterest, TikTok, and YouTube.

Sign up to join my *24/7 Self-help Library* for access to all of my helpful information, strategies, videos, and audio files, to learn and grow a self-hypnosis practice, reduce negative thoughts and feelings, bolster your physical and mental health with nutrition and lifestyle, and increase creativity and productivity—all on your schedule, by yourself, or for support between sessions. Use coupon code FREEMONTH to get the first month of your membership free as a thank-you for making it to the end of this book!

Endnotes

1. Chapter 1: You Versus Your Brain Morsella, E., Godwin, C. A., Jantz, T. K., Krieger, S. C., & Gazzaley, A. (2016). Homing in on consciousness in the nervous system: an action-based synthesis. *The Behavioral and brain sciences, 39*, e168. https://doi.org/10.1017/S0140525X15000643

2. Cheek, D. B. & LeCron, L. M. (1968). *Clinical Hypnotherapy*. New York: Grune and Stratton.

3. Lashley, K. S. (1956). Cerebral organization and behavior. *Proceedings of the Association for Research in Nervous and Mental Diseases 36*, 1–18.

4. Miller, G. A. (1962). *Psychology: The science of mental life*. Adams, Bannister, & Cox, 62.

5. Public statement by Ezequiel Morsella quoted in Kluger, J. (2015). Why you're pretty much unconscious all the time. *Time*. https://time.com/3937351/consciousness-unconsciousness-brain/

6. LeBlanc, A. (2001). The origins of the concept of dissociation: Paul Janet, his nephew Pierre, and the problem of post-hypnotic suggestion. *History of Science, 39*(1), 57–69. https://doi.org/10.1177/007327530103900103

7. Chapter 2: Birth of a Block Wolf, G. (1996). Steve Jobs: the next insanely great thing. *Wired.* https://www.wired.com/1996/02/jobs-2/

8. Chapter 3: How the Brain Works Dolan, B. (2007). Soul searching: A brief history of the mind/body debate in the neurosciences. *Neurosurgical Focus, 23*(1), 1–7. https://doi.org/10.3171/FOC-07/07/E2

9. Schacter, D. L. (1996). *Searching for Memory: The Brain, the Mind, and the Past.* New York: BasicBooks.

10. Barrett, L. F. (2017). *How Emotions Are Made: The Secret Life of the Brain.* New York: Mariner Books.

11. Schachter, S. & Singer, J. (1962). Cognitive, social, and physiological determinants of emotional state. *Psychological Review, 69*(5), 379.

12. Ekhtiari, H., Nasseri, P., Yavari, F., Mokri, A., & Monterosso, J. (2016). Neuroscience of drug craving for addiction medicine: from circuits to therapies. *Progress in Brain Research, 223*, 115–41.

13. Cole, M. W., Pathak, S., & Schneider, W. (2010). Identifying the brain's most globally connected regions. *NeuroImage, 49*, 3132–48. See also Sutherland M. T., McHugh M. J., Pariyadath V., & Stein E. A. (2012). Resting state functional connectivity in addiction: lessons learned and a road ahead. *NeuroImage, 62*(4), 2281–95. 10.1016/j.neuroimage.2012.01.117.

14. Cathartic method. *No Subject. Encyclopedia of Psychoanalysis.* https://www.nosubject.com/Cathartic_Method

15. Ginandes, C. S. & Rosenthal, D. I. (1999). Using hypnosis to accelerate the healing of bone fractures: a randomized controlled pilot study. *Alternative Therapies in Health and Medicine, 5(2),* 67–75.

16. Chapter 4: Hemispheric Asymmetries and Consciousness Morsella, et al. (2015).

17. Gazzaniga, M. S. (1988). *Mind Matters: How the Mind and Brain Interact to Create Our Conscious Lives.* Houghton Mifflin Company, in association with the MIT Press, Bradford Books.

18. Remmel, E. (2009). Brainstorming babies. *American Scientist, 97*(5), 413.

19. Chapter 5: Outsmarting the Brain Rosner, A. L. (1996). Laterality and Evolutionary Considerations of Visual M- and P-System Information Processing [Unpublished doctoral dissertation]. University of Memphis.

20. Dijkstra, N. & Fleming, S. M. (2023). Subjective signal strength distinguishes reality from imagination. *Nature Communications,* 14, 1627. https://doi.org/10.1038/s41467-023-37322-1

21. Chapter 6: Hypnotherapy Kihlstrom, J. F. (2023). Hypnosis and hypnotherapy. Update of Kihlstrom, J. F. (2016). Hypnosis. In Howard S. Friedman (ed.), *Encyclopedia of Mental Health (Second Edition)*, Oxford: Academic Press, 23–28. https://doi.org/10.1016/B978-0-12-397045-9.00180-4

22. Kihlstrom (2023).

23. Elman, D. (1964). *Hypnotherapy*. Glendale: Westwood Publishing Co.

24. Kihlstrom (2023), 218.

25. Chapter 7: Benefits of Hypnotherapy and Related Protocols Komesu, Y. M., Sapien, R. E., Rogers, R. G., & Ketai, L. H. (2011). Hypnotherapy for treatment of overactive bladder: a randomized controlled trial pilot study. *Female pelvic medicine & reconstructive surgery, 17*(6), 308–313. https://doi.org/10.1097/SPV.0b013e31823a08d9 See also Gonsalkorale, W. M., Houghton, L. A., & Whorwell, P. J. (2002). Hypnotherapy in irritable bowel syndrome: a large-scale audit of a clinical service with examination of factors influencing responsiveness. *The American Journal of Gastroenterology, 97*(4), 954–61. https://doi.org/10.1111/j.1572-0241.2002.05615.x

26. Montgomery, G. H., Bovbjerg, D. H., Schnur, J. B., David, D., Goldfarb, A., Weltz, C. R., Schechter, C., Graff-Zivin, J., Tatrow, K., Price, D. D., & Silverstein, J. H. (2007). A randomized clinical trial of a brief hypnosis intervention to control side effects in breast surgery patients. Journal of the National Cancer Institute, 99(17), 1304–12. https://doi.org/10.1093/jnci/djm106

27. Morrison J. B. (1988). Chronic asthma and improvement with relaxation induced by hypnotherapy. *Journal of the Royal Society of Medicine, 81*(12), 701–04. https://doi.org/10.1177/014107688808101207

28. Astin, J. A., Shapiro, S. L., Eisenberg, D. M., & Forys, K. L. (2003). Mind-body medicine: state of the science, implications for practice. *The Journal of the American Board of Family Practice, 16*(2), 131–147. https://doi.org/10.3122/jabfm.16.2.131

29. Hilgard, E. R., Hilgard, J. R. (1975). *Hypnosis in the Relief of Pain.* Los Altos, CA: Kaufman.

30. Facco, E. (2016). Hypnosis and anesthesia: back to the future. *Minerva Anestesiologica, 82*(12), 1343–56.

31. Chapter 8: Outcomes of an Unconscious-Oriented Approach Csikszentmihalyi, M. (1990). *Flow: The Psychology of Optimal Experience.* New York: Harper and Row.

32. Barrett (2017), 111

33. Wilson, T. D., Reinhard, D. A., Westgate, E. C., Gilbert, D. T., Ellerbeck, N., Hahn, C., Brown, C. L., & Shaked, A. (2014). Just think: The challenges of the disengaged mind. *Science, 345*(6192), 75–77. https://doi.org/10.1126/science.1250

34. Van Praet, D. (2017). Why negative thoughts are normal . . . and what you can do to lighten their load. *Psychology Today.* https://www.psychologytoday.com/us/blog/unconscious-branding/201705/why-negative-thoughts-are-normal

Printed in Great Britain
by Amazon